Simon Bullivant is a comedy writer and television producer – one of the creators of *They Think It's all Over* and *Never Mind the Buzzcocks*, and a key writer on shows including *Mock the Week* and *Argumental*.

He cut his comedy teeth on the radio, writing for shows such as *Week Ending* and *The News Huddlines*. During his radio years he also co-wrote a docudrama celebrating Batman's fiftieth anniversary as well as writing a comedy series about Britain's first costumed superhero, *Greywing*, starring Timothy Spall as the eponymous crime writer. He lives in London.

D0608980

THE BUMPER BOOK OF SLIGHTLY FORGOTTEN BUT NEVERTHELESS STILL GREAT BRITISH OLYMPIANS AND OTHER SPORTING HEROES

Constable • London

Constable & Robinson Ltd
55–56 Russell Square
London WC1B 4HP
www.constablerobinson.com

First published in the UK by Constable,
an imprint of Constable & Robinson Ltd, 2011

Copyright © Simon Bullivant, 2011
Illustrations © Nigel Winfield, 2011

The right of Simon Bullivant to be identified as the author of this
work has been asserted by him in accordance with the
Copyright, Designs and Patents Act 1988

All rights reserved. This book is sold subject to the condition
that it shall not, by way of trade or otherwise, be lent, re-sold,
hired out or otherwise circulated in any form of binding or cover
other than that in which it is published and without a similar condition
including this condition being imposed on the subsequent purchaser.

A copy of the British Library Cataloguing in
Publication data is available from the British Library

ISBN: 978-1-78033-230-7

Printed and bound in the UK

1 3 5 7 9 10 8 6 4 2

To my parents

I would like to thank my literary agent Gordon Wise and my editor Andreas Campomar; my agent Mike Sharland; producer Richard Wilson, 'the Silver Fox'; and all the many forgotten sportsmen and women from yesterday and tomorrow.

CONTENTS

FOREWORD

What do Nancy Giles, Gideon Halfbrass and Julius Frumney have in common? Were they the members of 'Velvet Cheese', one-hit wonders in the charts? Did they pitch up as contestants on *Big Brother 2*? Or were they three hapless victims of the Somaliland Stock Cube Scheme, which so scandalized high society in 1962? If you're uncertain as to the answer, the clue probably lies in this book's title: *The Bumper Book of Forgotten Sporting Heroes*. Because for every Ian Botham, George Best, Kelly Holmes or that Scottish cyclist with the big thighs there are countless great sportsmen and women whose names and feats have been sadly forgotten.

The reasons for this are rich and varied. Some competed in an age before mass communication, when cameras weren't around to record every detail. For others their moment of glory just happened to clash with a juicy episode of *Coronation Street*. It surely wasn't Maurice Dignam's fault that a fire broke out in the Rover's Return while he struck gold in the 1964 Underwater Hoop Plunge. And is it right that no one recalls the achievements of 'Scrapper' Watkins, one of our finest ragamuffin athletes and the first three-time winner of Sir Percival Neame's Obstacle Race for Urchins? Of course it's not. Who now remembers Tom Drake, dressage's first punk, who shocked the sport with his slashed jacket and the swear words on his hat?

Ron Driffield was an astounding athlete and only narrowly missed winning an Olympic medal. There is surely nobody who has ever flung the javelin further while surviving on a diet of nothing but egg and chips. Yet should the fact that he was a double murderer really diminish his prodigious sporting feats? Isn't it time to forgive and remember? The achievements of Maude Waveney, the plucky servant girl who bravely took half a day off work scrubbing kitchen floors to win a gold medal for folding bed-sheets in the first London games, surely deserve more respect; and why is the second Sir Henry Ardwell-Small, as brilliant a player of deck quoits as this country has ever produced, still so scandalously overlooked? Stripped of his title of Beekeeper Royal, for 80 years he's languished in obscurity. Time has also been unkind to 'Ample' Arthur Cartwright, whose brilliant football career was blighted by an obsession with archaeology. As to the pair of Cambridge students who triumphed in the three-legged goose-step at the Hitler Olympics – who remembers them? Can you name them? I don't suppose you can. Their names have been excised from all the best sports books – and most of the worst ones too.

Each and every one of these neglected sports stars deserves better.

Within the pages of this *Bumper Book* I have done my level best to redress the balance in their favour. You'll find here stirring feats of pluck, derring-do and countless other qualities the British imbibe with their mother's milk, all of which until now have been regrettably forgotten.

If I can return even just a few of these great athletes back to the public consciousness my work will have been worthwhile.

Simon Bullivant
2011

MAUDE WAVENEY

Bed-Making

One of the more surprising successes of the St Louis Olympics of 1904 had been the synchronized bed-sheet folding display. Crowds watched entranced as a hundred Missouri matrons in starched gingham dresses neatly folded enormous cotton sheets to a musical accompaniment. A bulky, new-fangled film camera recorded a few scratchy, speeded up seconds of the display, which would otherwise have been lost to posterity. A copy of the film became a treasured possession of E. Reginald Whipple, a travelling British cloth merchant, who was so impressed by what he saw that he felt compelled to persuade the London Olympic Organising Committee to include the event in their 1908 programme. They duly endorsed his suggestion, with a few amendments of their own, the most important one being the introduction of a competitive element.

Nowadays some might regard the fact that Whipple was sole supplier of cloth, flags and bunting to the London Olympics as an abuse of his position – which of course it was – but in Edwardian Britain it was regarded as perfectly acceptable for a gentleman to behave that way, and no shame was attached. For their part the organizers, under the redoubtable leadership of Sir Henry Rycroft, were less concerned about where the cloth came from than that the competition should attract the right sort of woman. After all, no self-respecting woman made her own bed in 1908 – or at least, no self-respecting woman admitted to it, and the committee believed it would be unseemly to expect any of the more well-bred ladies of the Empire to display their bed-making credentials in the heat of Olympic combat, and in public to boot. To spare their blushes, they decided to stiffen the entry requirements and ensure the competition was restricted to servant girls.

There was no shortage of women working in domestic service in the first decade of the twentieth century, and with 1907 Britain experiencing a servant glut, entry numbers for the bed-sheet folding event were expected to be high. But that, of course, brought its own problems. Who was to say that the contestants were genuine? Might not a lady of breeding dress down and pass herself off as a woman of an inferior class? It was a knotty issue, and the gentlemen of the 1908 Olympic Committee smoked many a fine cigar while ruminating over it.

To ensure that no subterfuge happened, and that no proper ladies, undercover suffragettes or bluestockings took part, Sir Henry Rycroft's team devised a series of tests to check that every competitor was the servant girl they claimed to be. The first element of this test was comparatively straightforward and involved nothing more than a close examination of the girl's hand for calluses. Only those with skin sufficiently hardened by years of scrubbing passed through. But that in itself was not a foolproof method. As Sir Henry pointed out to the committee, his own wife had rather rough fingers thanks to twenty years of light gardening – and Lady Maud had never made a bed nor scrubbed so much as a single floor in her life.

Any remaining doubts regarding the suitability of the competitors would only be resolved by the second part of the test, and it was here that the controversy ensued. For the recommendation of Sir Henry's committee was that each surviving girl who claimed to be a servant should be subjected to the traditional drunken fumble by an aristocrat. It was a fair test on the face of it, and seemingly foolproof. A domestic servant or indeed anyone from 'below stairs' would undoubtedly permit one of her social betters to fondle her behind the aspidistra, whereas the merest suggestion would naturally cause a lady of breeding to have a fit of the vapours and need reviving with smelling salts. It was the perfect solution. Unfortunately, no gentleman could be found – drunken or otherwise – who would be prepared to goose servant girls en masse. Even the guarantee of anonymity and a darkened room in which to commit the deed proved insufficient incentive. Discreet advertisements placed in gentlemen's magazines drew a frustrating blank. It looked as though the event would have to be dropped from the Olympic programme altogether, and this might have happened had it not been for the selfless eleventh-hour intervention by one of Europe's leading *roués*.

Baron Hargitay, a Hungarian nobleman of some wealth and ill repute, heard about the bed-making crisis and rushed to London, offering his considerable experience. The Baron had a notorious reputation amongst the titled families of Europe, and had left a trail of pregnant servant girls across the continent. Sir Henry offered him the job at once. No sooner had he thrown himself at the Organising Committee than Baron Hargitay threw himself at the young girls, and fondled the breasts and waists of over fifty servants in the spirit of international competition. A few dozen more he persuaded to sit on his knee, on the pretext of showing them how to play a traditional Hungarian dance on the piano.

The Olympic bed-making event, held at the Agricultural Hall in Islington, north London, was eventually won by Miss Maude Waveney, a nineteen-year-old girl from Accrington who made the regulation ten beds in a shade over fifteen minutes. It would have been a Lancashire one-two had not Miss Enid Stokes, a ruddy-faced chambermaid from Preston, been disqualified for ruckling one of the candlewick bedspreads.

Miss Waveney celebrated her gold medal by returning to Eaton Square, where she was in service to the Earl of Speyside, and scrubbing the scullery floor. By way of saying congratulations the Earl permitted her to sleep in until six o'clock the following morning.

Maude Waveney left domestic service in 1925, when she was thirty-six – and slightly too old to get married. She died in London, in 1974, aged eighty-five, her gold medal clutched in her bony, well-scrubbed hand.

SIR GEORGE INGOLLDS

Eighty-six-Yard Perambulation for Gentlemen of a Certain Girth

The origins of this highly specific event lie in the attempt by the London Olympic Organising Committee to introduce a race that could be entered, and won, by His Majesty King Edward VII. It was hoped, and indeed fully expected, that the ample-girthed King would enter the race and saunter to victory while his fellow competitors showed due deference and permitted the portly monarch to claim the victory laurels. Not for the first, nor indeed the last, time in the Olympic Games, things didn't go according to plan.

The 1908 London Games was only the second time that the Olympics had been held in a monarchy, and while King George of Greece had been present in 1896, he had chosen not to participate in any of the events. Fearing the same thing might happen to them, the London Olympic Organising Committee began trying their best to find a sport that would not only suit the sixty-six-year-old playboy monarch, but would guarantee him a gold medal. One of the more stately classes of yacht racing was their first suggestion, and initially met with royal approval, until the

5

King suffered a prolonged bout of seasickness off Cowes in 1906 and the idea was abandoned.

Nevertheless, the idea of a royal sporting event took root in the minds of Edward VII's closest advisors. It might prove to be a public relations winner. The bluff, bearded King was seldom seen outside of the royal palaces, and his subjects knew very little about him, except that he had a penchant for plumed hats, pretty girls, and could eat like a horse. Due to his great bulk, the King couldn't move at any great pace, which ruled him out of most athletics events. And that would have been that had it not been for the intervention of a member of the Buckingham Palace staff. In a discreet communication to the Organising Committee the Master of the King's Breakfast pointed out that under certain circumstances His Majesty could move like greased lightning. A tureen of steaming kedgeree or a mound of roasted quails only had to be placed on the breakfast table and the King would dash from his favourite armchair towards the food at blistering speed. The palace room, with the King's armchair at one end and the breakfast table at the other, was measured at exactly eighty-six yards long. The organizers had found their event. With one or two provisos in the rules, and a groaning table of braised ham or woodcock at the finish line, and it would be perfect for the King.

After some deliberations, the following rules were formulated. It was stipulated that for the race the gentleman's waist must measure no less than fifty-six inches in circumference, and that the participant should be unable to see his own feet when looking directly down from a standing position. At a generous fifty-seven and a half inches and with particularly dainty feet, King Edward VII comfortably met both requirements. But so too did Sir George Ingollds.

Ingollds was nominally a businessman, having made a fortune from gravel, although the vast majority of his time, not to mention his body, was devoted to the pursuit of food. Sir George trained for the Olympics as any other Edwardian gentleman would have done. This meant that he made no alterations to his undemanding schedule and spent much of the time asleep or playing roulette, occasionally both at the same time. Most importantly, though, his eating habits remained similarly unchanged, and in the run up to the games he dined almost exclusively on lobster and ptarmigan with all the trimmings, and swapped his sixty-inch waist trousers for a pair with an extra four inches. With scarcely a trace of irony he informed his fellow diners at the Alderman's Club that he wasn't planning to 'bust a gut', but in truth his overworked heart was firmly set on the silver medal. Ingollds had been made perfectly aware that the King would be one of the race entrants – indeed, the only one that mattered – and he did not need to be told that Edwardian etiquette expected that he should defer to his monarch and allow the King to waddle home for the gold.

But come the day, and come the hour, and to the huge embarrassment of the Games organizers, there was no sign of King Edward VII at all. Seven other corpulent gentlemen took their place on the starting line – including Beckmann, the forty-stone German, a jowly Frenchman called du Pont and, of course, Sir George Ingollds himself – but not one of them was the reigning monarch. Amidst chaotic scenes the event was delayed, during which time the venison at the finishing line first went cold, then was replaced, then went cold again and was replaced again. There was talk of postponing the race altogether, while more freshly cooked venison was prepared and a search party was sent out to try and locate the King. The assembled fat athletes were told to wait until His Majesty could be found. As soon as he arrived, they would start the race.

In the stadium, meanwhile, there was uproar. With the discus finished, and the eighty-six-yard perambulation yet to start there were no athletic events at all for the crowds to watch and, with loudspeakers still in their infancy, no adequate means of telling them what was – or wasn't – going on. While the Edwardian crowd watched, and smoked their heads off, the Games officials were in a complete flap. The 800-yard hurdles was cancelled, as was the one hundred yards race for matchgirls. Jeering began in the upper tiers, along with whistling – let's not forget these games took place in London, the Cockney home of whistling.

It was only the presence of the head of the International Olympic Committee (IOC) himself, Baron Pierre de Coubertin, that saved the day. 'Bollocks to ze King,' he told the organizers in his broken English. 'We will 'ave to run ze race wezzer he is here or not, no?' And with a twirl of his impressive French moustache he marched over to the by now famished fat men, grabbed the pistol from the starter, and set off the race.

It turned out to be all too easy for Sir George Ingollds who ambled, or rather strolled sweatily, to victory. Despite the handicap of a painful indigestion, due no doubt to not having eaten for a few hours, Sir George saw off the challenge of the fat German, a fat Belgian and two very fat Americans and took the gold medal, when he stomached the tape ahead of Monsieur du Pont.

And what of King Edward VII? None of the competitors, or indeed the crowd, was ever told. It wasn't until some years later, and the release of formerly classified documents, that it was revealed that the King had more pressing matters on race day, and had ended up spending the afternoon with Miss Kitty Wains, the so-called East Grinstead Bluebird. Had he just stopped for tea and cucumber sandwiches or had he shagged her? The documents didn't elaborate.

For Sir George Ingollds the eighty-six-yard perambulation was the limit of his sporting achievements. He died from acute poisoning less than three years later, after consuming over 200 oysters at his club on a sweltering hot day in June, 1911.

The eighty-six-yard perambulation for men of a certain girth has never subsequently been restaged at the Olympic Games.

WILFRED LONGSTAFF AND HERBERT RUNCIMAN

Three-Legged Goose-Step

It's no accident that the gold medal unexpectedly won by Longstaff and Runciman at the Berlin Olympics in 1936, has been lost to posterity. Their victory, in the one hundred metres three-legged race, came as something of an embarrassment to the British Olympic Association, and received almost no press coverage at the time. Of all the British gold medallists from Berlin, they were the only ones not invited on the open-top bus parade and the only ones not to go to Downing Street to meet Mr Baldwin. But the pair weren't so much ignored as shunned, and it is not difficult to understand why.

Wilfred Longstaff and Herbert Runciman, two graduates of Brasenose College Oxford from very different backgrounds, had first met at the University Athletics Club in 1931, when they found themselves paired for the intercollegiate three-legged race. Their first competition together was particularly inauspicious. Seconds after the start of the race Longstaff tripped over and cut his ankle, bringing Runciman down on top of him. It allowed the three-leggers

of University College to trot home to an easy victory. But instead of going their separate ways, the pair stunned the world of inter-varsity three-legged racing by staying together, and stormed back the following year when they became Oxford University champions. In addition, they beat Cambridge in the three-legged challenge by some distance, completing a rare double in 1933 when they won the Southern Counties three-legged race at White City stadium.

These were the great days of British three-legged racing. Peabody and Smith had run, ankles strapped, from Land's End to John o'Groats in 1932, and a high-jump record of three feet six and a bit had been set by the astonishing Tankerville twins at Motspur Park in the same year. Longstaff and Runciman were preparing their own assault on the record in 1934, when Runciman's mother fell ill. The pair abandoned their attempt and trotted to her bedside.

That might have been the limit for the two men had it not been for the unlikely news that reached Britain in 1934. Germany announced they were planning to introduce a three-legged race at the XI Olympiad. What, you might ask, did the continentals know about three-legged racing? Well, it's a little documented fact that Hitler himself was a keen devotee of the three-legged race, and even since becoming Reich Chancellor the testicularly challenged despot could on occasion be seen trotting around the Berchtesgaden with Joseph Goebbels or Heinrich Himmler lashed to his ankle. Although Longstaff and Runciman had not been tested against the world's best three-leggers, the Amateur Athletic Association was firmly convinced that the Oxford University men could triumph at the Games and threw all their considerable resources in the pair's direction. The two athletes were given their own running track upon which to practise, together with the help of Britain's first sports nutritionist, Mr Simper. Simper recommended a daily diet of suet puddings and beefsteak to help build up the athletes' trotting muscles, and Longstaff and Runciman duly obliged. The pair's prospects improved the following year when they learned that the highly respected Gruber brothers had taken a tumble at the American trials, and under the harsh selection procedure had failed to make the US team. On the other side of the world the Gupta twins, from Pondicherry in India, had been disqualified on the technicality that they were joined at the head, and thus had an unfair advantage. With two formidable rivals out of the way, the path seemed clear to British Olympic gold.

But then, dramatically at the eleventh hour, just before the opening ceremony, and with the team assembled in Berlin, the German Olympic Committee (or Deutsche Olympische Komitee to give them their proper name) had a change of heart. They announced that the three-legged race would not be run after all – but would instead be goose-stepped. It was disastrous news. Germany in 1936 was the goose-stepping capital of the world, and there could be only one outcome. The members of the British Olympic Committee (or Britische Olympische Komitee as they were called in the German newspapers) were appalled. When it was further stipulated that all athletes' ankles must be tied with German string, Lord Fishguard, the British chef de mission, demanded that the British pair be withdrawn immediately. Great Britain in those days was the manufacturer of the world's finest string, and Fishguard's Fibrous Filament the most peerless of all. A thunderous editorial in *The Times* insisted that no British athlete worth his salt would ever stoop to strap his ankles with foreign twine, and Winston Churchill spoke for over two hours in the House of Commons on the subject.

But Lord Fishguard, and the British political establishment, had reckoned without the determination of the British three-legged race champions, who weren't about to let five years of practice and two years of suet-pudding eating go up in smoke. Defying team orders they sneaked out of the Olympic village, bought a couple of plain singlets – their GB ones having been confiscated – and headed for the stadium. Their presence on the starting line was greeted with gasps from the knowledgeable German crowd, and even Hitler himself stopped ranting for a few minutes to watch the legendary ankle-coupled British athletes as they struggled to take off their tracksuits. After several minutes of awkward shuffling about, they eventually unstrapped themselves from each other, stripped down to their running kit, tied themselves back to one another again and prepared for the off.

The German paper *Die Zeit* had informed its readers that the race would be the equivalent of a walkover for the Fatherland, and that with the gold medal already certain, the crowd should concentrate its efforts on booing the decadent foreigners, and Jesse Owens in particular.

So the unexpected appearance of Longstaff and Runciman unsettled their predominantly German rivals. Dunwald and Krause began sweating, while the Ulmaier brothers forgot their stride pattern and started arguing with each other. The Belgian pair, meanwhile, fiddled with their unfamiliar German string.

As the gun sounded, all were left at the starting blocks as the English pair showed their competitors a clean pair of tied-together goose-stepping heels. Longstaff and Runciman led the race from gun to tape, beating the crack German outfit of Fischer and Grindlewald by some five metres.

It proved a hollow triumph. The British pair might have won an incredible gold medal but, as they trotted round the Olympic stadium to polite applause, found not a single British flag or banner waving to celebrate their victory. They discovered things were a lot worse when they attempted to return – untied by this point – to the Olympic village. The British section had been secured from the inside, the door handle tied firmly to a table leg – lashed, ironically, with British string. Locked out and shunned by their team-mates, the two men went their separate ways. Runciman returned to his native Yorkshire, while Longstaff went on holiday to the Dordogne.

The Amateur Athletic Association scrapped the three-legged race in 1937 – possibly as retaliation – and Longstaff and Runciman found themselves plying their trade on the underground three-legged race circuit in the south of France, until the Second World War broke out, killing millions of people and finishing three-legged racing for grown-ups for ever.

Both men served in the global conflict. Wilfred Longstaff spent the war years in the Pacific theatre, while Herbert Longstaff served in the army, losing a leg on Omaha Beach.

Longstaff died in a frozen gravel pit in 1955 while trying to rescue a wire-haired fox terrier which had got into difficulty, while Runciman passed away in a Leeds nursing home in 1972. The whereabouts of both men's gold medals is unknown.

TOM HIGGS

Shooting Germans (Three Positions)

History buffs will know that the Germans lost the First World War. (They lost the Second World War as well, but that's another story.) Yet is that any excuse for shooting defenceless people in the name of sport? Is an Olympic gold medal worth so much as a single life, let alone the 412 who lost theirs to provide sporting entertainment? In truth, the Shooting Germans (Three Positions) competition was considered controversial at the time. The event was introduced at the Antwerp Games of 1920 by Belgian hosts still smarting from the First World War. Yet as distasteful as it seems to modern sensibilities, the controversy at the time stemmed not from the mass carnage that ensued, nor whether points would be awarded for merely wounding, nor because only an outright kill would count towards the final score. No, the greatest debate centred on whether the competitors would use a French or a Hungarian rifle. Only after four fraught-filled days, which nearly split the Olympic brotherhood asunder, was a decision reached. Wounding, it was agreed, was a girl's sport and would count for nothing. As for the rifle, the French Nordiquay .22 small-bore rifle was given the nod. Not for the first time it was the French who got their way.

Of the event itself, held on a glorious summer day in the suburbs of Antwerp, the less said the better. A total of sixteen competitors, including a single British marksman, took to the range. In front of them, ranks of former German combatants who had yet to be repatriated lined up to be shot. After several hours of bloodthirsty shooting in the regulation three positions – prone, kneeling and standing – there were two competitors level in first place. Lars Nielsen, a Dane, and Henri Paroche, a local farmer, had slaughtered fifty-three Germans each. Competition rules necessitated a sudden death shoot-off to decide the champion, but so closely matched were the two sportsmen that it took a further five hours of shooting and eighty-three more dead Germans before Nielsen took an unexpected gold for Denmark. The Belgians were so upset at this setback that they cancelled two further shooting events – the rapid-fire free pigeon, and the wild tiger (military revolver). It is believed that the cancellation of these events saved the lives of countless pigeons, not to mention in the region of 200 Bengal tigers.

And what of Tom Higgs, the sole British competitor? Little is known about him, other than that he hailed from Leamington Spa and enjoyed dressing in medieval Japanese clothing. Most importantly of all, he worked at the British Consulate in Antwerp, where he was in charge of the stationery cupboard. Whilst on a trip to Brussels to buy some 2B pencils and turquoise-coloured ink, Higgs struck up a conversation with Colonel Reddings, a fellow Briton who was bulk-buying elastic bands. Reddings, an ex-pat gun enthusiast and sole member of the Keep the War Going

Society, had heard about the upcoming shooting event and determined that with Germans to be killed Britain should field an entrant. He would volunteer himself, he explained, were it not for his shaky left arm. Despite the fact that he'd never wielded anything more dangerous than a samurai sword, the impressionable Higgs readily agreed and, as he was owed four days' holiday by the Consulate, put his name forward.

As it turned out, under the pressure of Olympic combat, Higgs proved to have an even shakier arm than the colonel. His bullets sprayed all over the arena, and by the end of the competition he'd only managed to kill eight Germans. The record books say eight, although this total was swelled by the addition of a photographer, a programme-seller and a fellow competitor. Olaf Steingaard, the crack-shot Norwegian marksman, duly became the first winner of a posthumous bronze medal.

Tom Higgs returned to the Consulate where he worked – quietly and anonymously – until an autumn day in 1923 when he popped out to buy some lever-arch files and never came back.

This was the first and only time that humans have been deliberately killed in an Olympic sporting contest, and the event had been removed from the calendar by 1924. An attempt by the Germans to introduce a Shooting Belgians (Three Positions) event in 1936 was wisely overruled by the IOC.

GENTLEMAN JACK PERKINS

Heavyweight Boxing

The late 1890s were heady days for British boxing: the Marquess of Queensbury, having vanquished Oscar Wilde, could devote himself to the sport, while a burly Cornishman, Bob Fitzsimmons, was the undisputed heavyweight champion of the world. Fitzsimmons is rightly regarded as a legend in the sport, but in his day he had to contend with an equally talented British rival, a man who is all but forgotten today: Gentleman Jack Perkins.

Jack Perkins was born in rural Nottinghamshire, and into a life of wealth and privilege, in 1873. His grandfather, a chandler from Newark, had invented the 'Grinding Colin' – a cumbersome machine which separated tallow fats – and had been created the first Earl Perkins for services to the candle industry.

In 1891 Jack left Harrow and went up to Cambridge to study tallow blending at Oriel, as was then the fashion among the candle-manufacturing classes. It didn't take too long for Jack to show an aptitude with his fists, when he savagely laid into a tutor who had spotted that the young man was unable to read or write. The college authorities acted at once and, despite being a scion of moneyed stock, the boy was expelled.

His family were most disappointed – they'd long suspected Jack wouldn't be suited to running the family business, but now came to realize that such intemperate behaviour would jeopardize his chances of joining the clergy. It shouldn't be forgotten that this was some time before the age of the great boxing vicars, men like the vicar of Chorley, the Reverend 'Sugar' Martin Danderfoot, who instructed his parishioners to jab for Jesus. Disappointed at this rejection, Jack left the family home – ironically on Boxing Day, 1892 – and never returned. Cut off from a fortune estimated to be in excess of eighty million pounds – which was a lot of money in 1892 – Jack joined the circus and began making a few coppers in the sideshow. The India Rubber Man, the Trapeze Artist, the Bearded Lady – Jack gave them all a pummelling with his rock-hard fists. 'Wild Bill' Coggleshall, the one-armed lion tamer, was hospitalized. It was the custom in those days for boxers to adopt nicknames, and as he was the son of a lord, Perkins was given the title 'Gentleman Jack'. He soon made a name for himself with his luxurious mutton-chop whiskers, blue-blooded reputation and a boxing style that bordered on brute savagery. Perkins also gained a reputation as a speed merchant, as some of his contests had been known to finish in under sixty-three rounds.

By 1895, having defeated all comers, Jack decided he would leave for America and challenge for the heavyweight championship of the world. But his arrival there was a disaster. No sooner had he disembarked than Jack was presented with a writ from another boxer, Gentleman Jim Corbett, who claimed a copyright on the nickname Gentleman. The Nottinghamshire boxer found he was unable to box, tied up in red tape and legal matters he could neither read nor understand, while his fellow Englishman Bob Fitzsimmons defeated Corbett and became undisputed heavyweight champion. By the time the case was concluded, in 1902, Jack's best days were behind him. He'd had a few fights, as 'Plain' Jack Perkins, beating such turn-of-the-century notables as Colorado John Jackson, James J. James, Fat Ernie Donohue and Pinky Bastard, but boxing had moved on and he never got a crack at the world champion.

In 1904, Jack was contacted by the British Consul in Missouri, Sir Clifford Napper, who suggested that he compete for Britain at the forthcoming Olympics to be held in St Louis. When someone finally read him the letter, Gentleman Jack agreed. Despite his growing disillusionment with the sport, he spent the next few months diligently preparing for the games. The dumb-bell lifting and similar Herculean feats worked wonders. Jack reached the heavy-weight final with ease, having bludgeoned three opponents into submission. In all probability he would have beaten Sam Berger, the last American left standing, had it not been for the intervention of the Olympic supremo himself, Baron Pierre de Coubertin. While the Baron was delighted to see an English nobleman at the games, the news that Gentleman Jack had once boxed for money, and pocketed winnings of four shillings and sixpence, caused de Coubertin deep distress. As a professional, Jack had no right to compete at the games, the Baron informed him, and slapped him across the face with his silk gloves for good measure. What reply Gentleman Jack made is uncertain, although we can presume he was upset as he punched de Coubertin squarely on the chin, knocking off the Baron's top hat and dislodging two of his teeth.

Flat broke, disinherited and distressed, Perkins drifted back into his former life. He joined a two-bit circus in Densmore, Ohio, and once again began boxing for money. In 1906 he fought five times, earning just over twelve dollars. Gentleman Jack Perkins never returned to England, and after 1903 all reference to him was completely removed from *Burke's* and *Debrett's*. Nevertheless, his final years were happy ones. In 1910 he married Sonia the sword-swallower, although they subsequently discovered she was unable to bear children.

Their joy was short-lived. In 1913, on a trip to California to buy some performing bears, Gentleman Jack Perkins suffered a massive coronary and died. At the funeral service in Densmore, his coffin was carried – rather lopsidedly – by a number of circus performers, and a boxing exhibition match was held in his honour. There were no candles, by request.

DOUG AND DEMELZA DAVIDSON

Mixed Luge

Doug and Demelza Davidson were Britain's first great Winter Olympians, and dominated the long defunct mixed luge event in the inter-war years. It's a shame, then, that their feats are nowadays all but forgotten, their achievements shrouded in secrecy.

Douglas Clement Davidson was born in Peterborough in 1908. His father, Douglas senior, was reputed to own the finest collection of straw hats in all of East Anglia. Young Douglas saw very little of these hats – which were kept under lock and key – and even less of his father, who scoured the globe in search of exotic raffia headgear. Sadly for the boy – and indeed Mrs Davidson – he was lost at sea in 1917 along with a number of fellow hat enthusiasts when their boat was torpedoed by a German submarine. Douglas fervently hoped that his father had survived, but he hadn't. He was dead. All life, and all hats, had been lost.

The widowed Mrs Davidson went into a steep decline that culminated in complete madness. Believing that another Ice Age was imminent she built an enormous artificial ski ramp in the back garden before she was led off to a padded cell. But his mother's insanity proved to be a blessing for young Douglas, who enjoyed all the benefits of a 300-foot ski ramp just outside his back door, and in 1922 he won the Cambridgeshire downhill skiing championships on his home slope. By 1924 he was national champion, and set off to the first Winter Olympics in Chamonix with high hopes. There was only one problem. As ridiculous as it sounds today, in 1924 there were no alpine skiing events on the Winter Olympic programme, and for Douglas Davidson it was a wasted journey. He did try his hand at the Ice Quoits, there being no other British representative in that particular event, but he finished well down the field. What did attract him, however, was the 16-man bob, a hugely cumbersome and impractical discipline which has not survived to the present day. It was difficult enough to get sixteen bobbers to coordinate their sliding and pushing, and it proved impossible for the mammoth sleds to negotiate the tight bends. None of the twelve crews completed the course and the event was scrapped.

Douglas returned home crestfallen, and for several years had nothing to do with winter sports – the only exception being ice yachting, a short-lived craze on the Norfolk Broads in the bitterly cold winter of 1927. The following year he went to work at the Ministry of Agriculture, in the Minced Beef department. It was in 1930, at a tea dance to celebrate British Celery Week, that he met his future wife. Demelza Gooding was an assistant tea lady with her own enamelled tea urn and cake trolley, and after a whirlwind romance lasting three-quarters of an hour – which is pretty fast, even by whirlwind romance standards – the pair got married.

Demelza had been born and raised in Kenya on a tea plantation. Her father had brought the family back to

England in 1919, believing there was a fortune to be made in rose-hip syrup. But no sooner had he arrived and invested his money than the bottom fell out of the market, and the Goodings lost everything. Thousands like him, who'd put their money into cough linctus, went to the wall. To make ends meet Demelza took a job at the Ministry. Her long dreary years there passed without incident – save for the day in 1926 when she spilt scalding hot tea down Mr Baldwin's trousers during a state visit by the King of Romania.

After their marriage the young couple honeymooned in Switzerland where a local couple introduced them to the delights of the luge, a sort of fancy toboggan. After two weeks of sex and luging the happy couple returned to Doug's childhood home, Davidson Hall – otherwise known as 'The Poplars', 14 Girton Avenue. They repaired the rotting ski slope and turned it into a gigantic luge ramp. In 1932, and again in 1933, 'The Poplars' hosted the British Mixed Luging Championships. The Davidsons won the title both times beating their only rivals – the Blatchfords from Number 12. By 1934 Doug had risen in the Ministry, becoming quite an authority on pork sausages. Nevertheless, in January 1934 he resigned his post, cancelled the championships and headed off to the Alps with Demelza. Word was afoot that Germany would be including a luge event – possibly for husbands and wives – at the 1936 Winter Games, to be held at Garmisch-Partenkirchen. But despite almost two years of constant luging, and some intermittent sex, their practice came to naught. Though they marched around the stadium and shivered at the opening ceremony, clutching their home-made toboggan, that was the limit of Doug and Demelza Davidson's involvement in the 1936 Winter Olympics. The cunning Germans had decided not to include it on the programme.

Worse news was to greet them when they returned home. The ski slope at 'The Poplars' had mysteriously burned down and the fire spread to Number 14. Like their former house, the pair of them were gutted. The following week they moved to Scotland, bought a small hotel in Perthshire, and began quietly practising for the 1940 games away from the limelight.

Thanks to the Second World War, of course, the Winter Olympics of 1940 never happened, and that might have been the last we'd have heard of Doug and Demelza Davidson had it not been for a footnote in an obscure document, released some fifty years later under the Freedom of Information Act. It seems that in the bleak winter of 1940 the Davidsons were summoned to Downing Street for a top secret meeting with none other than Winston Churchill himself. The free world was in dire peril, Churchill told them. What the allies needed, he went on, was someone to lead the British Army's proposed new Luging Light Infantry. The Prime Minister envisaged a small unit of elite troops who could luge their way across Europe and really stick it up the Germans. It seems Demelza suggested that she and Doug could better work on their own, secretly helping people by luging them off to safety, probably in Switzerland. Churchill agreed.

The Davidsons left for Switzerland immediately, and spent almost the entire duration of the war in the alpine region. Who knows how many countless lives they saved? It's impossible to say. The top secret document didn't mention any figures.

Doug and Demelza Davidson were last seen alive in

February 1943 in Brevy-sur-Mont, a tiny Swiss border village with a rather unusual water pump in the town square. It was Monday morning at 11.15. Certainly no later than half eleven. They checked out of their hotel, luged off into the snow and were never seen again.

In 1956, to commemorate Doug and Demelza Davidson's contribution to the successful fight against Nazi tyranny, a medal was struck in their honour – the British Empire Luging Cross. Only two of them were ever awarded, to the Davidsons who, alas, never collected them. It was the most important medal either of them ever won.

ARCHIE MCGILLIVRAY

Ballooning

Although he represented Britain at the Los Angeles Games of 1932, the only occasion on which ballooning has featured as an Olympic sport, Archie McGillivray is best remembered as a never-say-die golfer, who twice came within a whisker of winning the Open.

Born in 1895, in Largs on the Ayrshire coast, Archie was raised in a golfing family. His father Alex was a freelance green-keeper with extremely prominent ears, and while Mr McGillivray had a flair for the game he had very poor business sense. With scarcely two halfpennies to rub together, young Archie was packed off to St Lachlan's Academy for Wee Bairns Whose Folks Have Nae Cash in nearby Troon. The school had a poor academic record, but it did offer the best under-elevens' caddying course on the west coast of Scotland. By the time he'd left, in 1908, Archie had learned to do a good deal more than simply carry clubs for rich folk. He'd mastered the game of golf.

In 1914, having acquired a trim moustache, he qualified for the Open Championship at Prestwick, and for three-and-a-half rounds headed the field. Had it not been for a catastrophic error at the final hole, when his ball plugged in a cowpat, he might have held on to win. As it was the great Harry Vardon pipped him by a stroke. Archie consoled himself with the knowledge that he'd go one better the following year, but it was not to be. The next few years were consumed by matters somewhat more important than golf, as war gripped the world. Like so many other brave young men Archie McGillivray enlisted in the army. He joined the Fourteen Ayrshire and Troon Light Infantry, one of Scotland's finest golfing regiments. The Fourteen Ayrshire had last seen action at Ladysmith, when their charge directly at the enemy guns armed only with putters had earned them the nickname 'The Straight Down the Middles'. The regiment had been completely wiped out. At Ypres the regiment almost befell a similar fate. Archie was lucky – he only sustained serious injuries – and was sent home to convalesce for the remainder of the conflict.

It was during this time that he suddenly acquired a passion for ballooning, although no one knows why. But no sooner was he back on his feet again than Archie scraped together all his meagre savings, bought an enormous balloon, huge wicker basket, ropes, bags of sand and a puncture repair kit, and was soaring over the hills and glens of Scotland. His golf game suffered, but Archie McGillivray could console himself that in 1922 and again in 1923 he was the British Ballooning Champion.

The 1920s were a time of great change in Britain. In addition to all the strikes, unrest and social upheaval, the vinegar giants Sarson's discovered that people were using less of their product on their chips. So in 1924, as a publicity gimmick to promote the use of vinegar, Sarson's sponsored the Sheffield to Shanghai balloon race for the Sarson's

Vinegar Cup. After a race lasting several months Archie triumphed, beating off Hildegard Fleumel, the legendary German balloonist, and several other golfers who'd taken up the sport. Offered a lift home, on a slow boat from China, Archie politely declined. He'd arrived by balloon, and by balloon he'd return. Sadly, his journey home was a disaster. The six-foot-high solid silver trophy was too heavy for the frail wicker basket, and half-way across the Himalayas it plunged through the floor, where it presumably lies today, covered in snow. Only his quick wits saved Archie, who had to cling to the sides of the basket for several thousand miles before he reached the safety of Kent.

In 1929 the ballooning world was agog. The rumours that the Americans planned to introduce the sport at the forthcoming Olympics, to be held in Los Angeles, had turned out to be true. There would be two classes – freestyle and Greco-Roman ballooning, better known to us these days as hot air ballooning.

In Britain, Archie McGillivray was reckoned to be unbeatable. Writing in *Dirigible News*, Tim Farmiloe, Guernsey's leading balloon journalist, described the Scot as the greatest aeronauticist the world had ever seen. They might as well hang a gold medal round his neck now, he contended. But the British ballooning press were notoriously insular in the 1930s, none more so than Farmiloe, a man whose travels had only taken him as far as Jersey. They had all reckoned without Hildegard Fleumel – for whom defeat in the Sheffield to Shanghai race still rankled – and Magnus Gustafsson, the Swedish playboy who had revolutionized the staid world of Scandinavian ballooning. Throughout 1930 and 1931 he posted impressive results, winning the Norway Classic and the Crosse & Blackwell Shield, a rival vinegar-sponsored balloon race. But Gustafsson's showmanship was to be his undoing. Arriving in the States ahead of the games he abandoned the official Swedish Olympic balloon in favour of his own personal craft, shaped like an enormous phallus. The notoriously puritanical Americans, citing an obscure loophole in the constitution relating to penis-shaped inflatables, impounded the craft and burnt it in a great big fire.

With the Swede absent there were only nine starters for the big race and, taking advantage of the favourable thermals, Archie soon gusted into a sufficiently strong lead that he felt free to enjoy some chicken sandwiches, a rare treat in the Olympic cauldron. By the halfway mark only the American, Bud Weingartner, could keep pace with the blustery Scot.

It was on the homeward leg that disaster struck Archie McGillivray and left the event mired in controversy. He was just ten miles from the finish and enjoying the scenery when he felt the balloon dropping through the sky towards terra firma. Archie skilfully piloted his craft to the ground, but any chance of the gold medal had gone, and he watched in frustration as Bud Weingartner, waving a twelve-bore shotgun and a king-sized flag, crossed the finish line to a tumultuous reception. Great sportsman that he was Archie applauded his rival's success without any bitterness, even when tests indicated that the plethora of holes in his downed balloon had almost certainly been caused by a twelve-bore shotgun. 'That's ballooning' was Archie's only comment. The British team were not so phlegmatic and, using the spent shell cases as evidence of Weingartner's wrongdoing, appealed the result. The US team insisted that their balloonist had merely exercised every American's right to bear arms – a defence that was at once rejected by the Olympic Committee, and Bud Weingartner was disqualified. The following morning, after a baying torchlit parade surrounded their headquarters, the same committee reinstated Weingartner's gold medal and American honour was satisfied.

Archie McGillivray returned to Scotland where he continued to race and opened a ballooning shop in his home town of Largs. Within a matter of months the enterprise had collapsed, however; the great days of ballooning were over.

He lived quietly in the town for the next twenty years, only coming to the public's attention in 1959, when he was knifed by teddy boys in a scuffle at a bus stop. His ashes were sprinkled at sea the following year, and again in 1961, after it was discovered that there'd been a mix up at the crematorium and another person's ashes had been dropped into the Atlantic.

GERTRUDE TRELAWNEY-FERRIS

Croquet; Cricket; Golf; Figure Skating; Tennis; Rugby; Swimming

Along with her more famous compatriot Lottie Dod, Gertrude Trelawney-Ferris was one of the early pioneers of women's sport in Great Britain. As well as being an out-standing athlete she was also witty, exhilarating, intelligent and fat, making her an all-rounder in both senses.

'Golden Gertie', as she was later dubbed, was born in 1883 – or possibly 1884. It was never established when, or for that matter where. She was found on a chilly January night in Reigate, on a bed of non-deposit empties, outside Benbow's the off licence. In the summer of 1886, at the age of two – or three – she was adopted by a Mr and Mrs Trelawney-Ferris, a posh but eccentric couple who lived in a gypsy caravan. Although stern, they gave their adoptive daughter a thorough education. The girl learned science, art, literature, glassblowing, how to fix a broken caravan wheel and, most of all, sport. In 1899 Gertrude gained her first trophy when she was crowned schoolgirl croquet champion of Sussex, and with a cup on the mobile mantelpiece turned her attention to cricket. Bounding

across the square, her 4 ft 9, fifteen-stone frame was a sight to behold. But her physical appearance paled into insignificance next to her talent. Playing for Sussex Ladies in June 1900 at the age of sixteen – or possibly seventeen – she scored 103 not out and took eight for forty-six against the touring Australian Cabinet Makers XI. It was the first time an Aussie furniture-making outfit had ever been skittled out by a team of women cricketers, and the result rocked the world of cricket – and woodcraft – to its foundations.

But cricket wasn't Gertrude's only interest. She was also quite useful at golf. In 1902, aged eighteen or nineteen, she went round Sandwich golf course in sixty-eight strokes, beating the course record for a fat young lady. Of course, these were very much the formative years of women's sport. Tennis was still in its infancy; the women's FA had not been founded; and no member of the fair sex had swum the length of Lake Windermere. Gertrude put that right in 1903.

But Edwardian society rather frowned on pioneering sportswomen like Gertie – even ones with double-barrelled surnames. They believed she, and other women like her, should be at home providing their husbands with a minimum of seven children. Certainly not playing water polo, jiu-jitsu or attempting nine-dart checkouts – which, incidentally, she first achieved in 1904. Nor trying to play rugby union. It was in early 1905 that Gertie smuggled herself into a trial match for Harlequins rugby club. Things went well until her false beard was pulled off in a ruck, after which her three tries, two conversions and a drop goal were annulled and she was frog-marched from the ground.

It was in the following summer, however, that Gertrude Trelawney-Ferris achieved lasting notoriety. Playing in the ladies semi-final at Wimbledon, and wearing a calico dress of her own design, she did the unthinkable and bared her ankles. Uproar followed and the umpire abandoned the match. The following day there was an indignant leader column in *The Times*, and Sir Henry Campbell-Bannerman, the Prime Minister, made an emergency statement in the house. To make matters worse, her Border collie, Wilf, was hit by a tram that same afternoon.

Poor Gertie's world began falling apart. Her figure-skating bronze at the 1908 Olympics went largely unreported and she was dropped from the England Ladies cricket team. Gertrude's stunning watercolours, which once took pride of place at the Summer Exhibition, were now rejected by the Royal Academy. No one wanted to know about her quick-setting epoxy resin, discovered while she'd been dabbling with her chemistry set, while the cheeky music hall duet she recorded with Enrico Caruso, 'O Cornetto Mio' – 'Oh My Trumpet' – merely gathered dust on the shelves.

But in 1912 Gertrude hit upon what she regarded as a brilliant sporting venture which, although she couldn't have known it at the time, was to prove her last. She would try something that no one had ever attempted before and circumnavigate the Isle of Wight in a pedalo. All went swimmingly until the little craft ran into a rather big ship – the *Titanic* – steaming through the Solent on her ill-fated maiden voyage. Hauled from the choppy waters by a passing Norwegian schooner, Gertie immediately announced her retirement from sport. Unfortunately the crew didn't understand a word of English and she had to repeat her statement to the pressmen waiting on Ventnor Harbour.

At the age of twenty-eight, or quite possibly twenty-nine, Gertrude Trelawney-Ferris was at a crossroads in her life.

Uncertain what path to take next she went trekking and shooting caribou in Canada. While there she met a similarly disaffected Burmese prince called Ipom, who had a penchant for fat ladies. In 1916, after a courtship lasting two years, the couple returned to Rangoon and set up home in one of Ipom's sumptuous palaces. Gertie adjusted to the luxury of Burmese court life and spent the next few years raising seven children. Had it not passed away some years earlier, Edwardian society would have been pleased.

Gertrude did come back to Britain on one occasion, in 1933 when, aged forty-nine or fifty, she ran in a half-marathon at Basingstoke and delivered a lecture on the cultivation of walnuts, though not at the same time. She died in 1938 whilst holing in one at Rangoon Golf Club's par three fourteenth. Or possibly fifteenth.

FRANKIE SWOOP

Very Modern Pentathlon

It was Frankie Swoop's good fortune to find himself in the right place at the right time – just a few miles from Mexico when that very country was hosting the Olympic Games. Perhaps it was all just too good to be true, because in the end that fortuity came to nothing. But as Frankie said at the time and repeated many times later, 'Chill out man. It's cool.'

Frankie Swoop was born in Stoke-on-Trent during the long winter of 1947. His father, Frank senior, was an honorary member of the Lard Council, and advised his son that a future beckoned in the world of rendered pork fat. But lard held few attractions for go-ahead men in the 1960s, and young Frankie was no exception. Instead he went to work at a trendy new boutique in Burslem High Street called 'Lord Nigel's Gear' where he sold tight trousers, sheepskin coats, faux military jackets and smoking paraphernalia. There was a restless spirit in Frankie Swoop, however, and when he'd gathered up enough savings he waved goodbye to Stoke and headed off for the west coast of America. His initial movements are not documented. What is known for certain is that in 1967, during the infamous 'Summer of Love', he enrolled at the Far Out University of California to take a degree in Cool Things. How much studying Frankie did at this institution is not recorded either, as the students spent most of their time rioting or engaged in lengthy sit-ins, and all the relevant documentation was destroyed when the National Guard ransacked the building in 1969.

What we know of Frankie's movements in this critical period is largely thanks to his correspondence – namely the erratic postcards he sent to his parents in Stoke. In early 1968, he informed them that the course was getting 'too heavy' and that he planned to go hitchhiking around California to try and 'find himself'. This message was written on the back of a postcard depicting a giant redwood. Some weeks later came a card with a Mexican stamp and a picture of the monastery of Santa Vera de la Cruz. The message was almost illegible. What little Mr and Mrs Swoop could make out was that the sun was 'friggin' hot, man' and that there was some 'killer weed'. There was no further communication from Frankie for six months.

But, postcards or not, it would appear that Frankie's soul-searching travels took him as far south as Mexico City, just as the Olympic Games were about to begin. This much we know for sure – after all, the evidence exists in the TV pictures. He's shown marching around the stadium with his fellow team members behind the British flag, in the row behind David Hemery. You can easily recognize Frankie Swoop as he's the only member of the party wearing open-toe sandals and smoking. What exactly he was smoking we can only guess, but quite how a feckless Stoke-born layabout should find himself in the British Olympic team deserves some explanation.

Thanks to the development of satellite technology the pictures of the Mexico Games could be beamed live into living rooms around the world, morning, noon and night. They would be the first truly modern Olympics. In keeping with this breakthrough the IOC recommended that a new event be introduced to reflect the spirit of the age. Several popular sports – like golf, tennis and shinty – put themselves forward for inclusion. But after some deliberation the committee decided on a sport of their own, the Very Modern Pentathlon, to run alongside the much more old-fashioned Modern Pentathlon. Unlike its traditional counterpart, which included shooting, fencing, riding, swimming and running, the Very Modern Pentathlon would be a radical departure. Chopper riding would replace the swimming, while the fencers would use épées instead of foils. Some felt the changes hadn't gone far enough, but they were slapped down by Avery Brundage, the autocrat who ran the IOC almost single-handedly in 1968. For Frankie Swoop, it was the ideal sport. He'd picked up fencing when he worked at 'Lord Nigel's Gear'; learned to shoot at the Far Out University by aiming at cut-outs of 'pigs' and 'the Man'; was the fastest chopper rider in Stoke; and even with marijuana-clogged lungs could run a bit too – especially if he was being chased by 'pigs' or 'the Man'. The horse riding was the unknown quantity.

The event was held over five consecutive days, and after the first two Frankie found himself handily placed. He somehow managed to hold on to his horse on day three, while several of his better placed rivals fell off, and following an impressive display on the chopper was leading the field after four days of competition. That's when it all went wrong for Frankie Swoop. Instead of going back to the Olympic village to get a good night's sleep and prepare for the biggest day of his life, with the possibility of a gold medal and sporting immortality at the end of it, Frankie headed off to downtown Mexico City to get hammered on cheap tequila. In his defence, he'd done this for the previous four nights, and his form had not been affected. But on this occasion it seems he bumped into some fellow students from the Far Out University, who had a camper van laden with top quality weed, and Frankie spent the night smoking himself into oblivion. By the time he emerged, three days later, not only his event, but the Olympic Games themselves, were history.

Conspiracy theories have raged since then that Frankie Swoop was 'nobbled' – perhaps by Mladenov, the Bulgarian athlete in second place, who might have tampered with Frankie's tequila or slipped him some extra strong marijuana. Although it's always tempting to look at an excuse for British failure, and to blame others for our own shortcomings, Frankie hardly needed much persuading to veer from the straight and narrow. When he was questioned later by concerned team officials, Frankie merely shrugged his shoulders, grinned and gave them his customary 'Chill out man. It's cool.'

By the mid 1970s Frankie Swoop was back in England and living in a squat in Runcorn, Cheshire. Together with some disaffected local youths he formed a punk rock band, Human Skin Soup. The group turned out to be awful, folded after only one gig, and the 'Runcorn Sound' became the shortest-lived phenomenon of Jubilee Year. He made one brief stab at getting back into sport, when he applied for the vacant chairmanship of the British Chopper Biking Federation. Tragically, the federation had folded some two years earlier, in 1975, when chopper bikes went out of fashion, and the letter was returned to his squat. When the bailiffs moved in, a few weeks later, Frankie Swoop had flown the nest.

DR WILLIAM THORNAGE

Weights and Measures Fact-Finding
Commission of 1896

William Thornage, a science graduate and fellow of King's College, London, never threw a javelin, nor ran the half-mile, rowed the Thames or mounted a penny farthing in competition, fun or anger. Yet despite his lack of athletic credentials he remains a pivotal figure in British sport, a man who shaped the destinies of countless athletes.

There were no British representatives present in the Paris Convention of 1894, when Baron Pierre de Coubertin announced his intention to stage the inaugural Olympic Games in Greece two years hence. Franco-British relations were not at their happiest, and the Baron had not seen fit to send an invite to any of the sporting bodies in Great Britain. Nevertheless, as one of the world's pioneering sporting nations, one which could lay claim to the origins of football, cricket, golf, rugby and tennis, it was only natural that the United Kingdom would wish to attend the Athens games – invited or not – and come home with a ship full of gold medals. There was only one problem. The International Olympic Committee had been established under continental rules, and Baron de Coubertin had decreed that all the events would be calibrated using the metric system.

This news sent shock waves through the British sporting establishment. Not a single member of any athletic body – or indeed anybody in the entire country – had the foggiest understanding of how long a metre was, nor how much a kilogramme weighed. There was talk that the metre was near enough a yard – but was it a bit longer, or a bit shorter? Or was the whole thing just a damned Frenchy trick dreamed up to annoy the British, and there was no difference at all? After all, why have something that was like a yard but wasn't a yard when a yard was perfectly good enough? As to the kilogramme, the best minds in the land were at a complete loss.

The natural thing to do might have been to contact the French ambassador, who could no doubt have supplied fulsome explanations along with quantities of metric tapes and weights. But such a request was very difficult to make as it fell foul of the 'Don't Ask The French For Anything' Act of 1879. This left the athletes, and the officials, in a quandary. How could a runner hope to prepare for an 800-metre race, if he had no idea how far he was expected to run? There was talk, for a while, of tactfully withdrawing from the games altogether. Then William Thornage came to the rescue.

In May 1895, Dr Thornage, a keen traveller and Hellenophile, answered an advertisement in *London Life* for a travelling companion to explore the ruins of the Greek mainland. The person who had placed the advert was looking for 'a bachelor who likes a smoke, has a good sense of humour, and is prepared for adventure'. Dr Thornage, an unmarried fun-loving devotee of the pipe, responded to the advert. A few days later, and much to his surprise, he was met with a delegation from the British Olympic Association (BOA). It was not their intention to go to Greece and see the sights or paint watercolours and write airy-fairy poetry, they informed him. What Britain wanted most, in this hour of need, was for someone to go to Greece, make a reconnaissance of the Olympic stadium and – most crucially – bring back some bona fide metric measuring instruments. After they agreed to pay his fare and considerable expenses, Dr Thornage consented to go.

Throughout June and most of July the doctor travelled throughout Greece, sending back reports on the state of the Olympic stadium and the other assorted preparations. Finally, in late July, on the reverse of a postcard depicting the ruins of Delphi he informed the BOA that he'd acquired a set of metric instruments and was sailing for home. Unfortunately, due to an entirely innocent misunderstanding with a vicar's daughter on the boat-trip back, the metre ruler was snapped in half by an irate clergyman and thrown overboard, leaving Dr Thornage with only a set of bronze weights and a black eye to show for his long holiday. He took the next boat back to Greece, and in early September finally acquired a second metre rule. It was a frustrating time for the doctor, as the shop was out of stock and it took several weeks for their French suppliers to refurnish them with metric rulers.

This time he managed to bring back the wooden stick unbroken. Dr Thornage duly handed it over to the British Olympic Association amidst a little pomp and ceremony, after which the metre rule was sent off to be copied, mass-produced and distributed across the clubs and universities of the land. With that, William Thornage's involvement with the Olympic movement came to an end. He didn't return to Greece the following year, when the first Games were held, or indeed at any time after, despite living to a ripe old age.

In due course, it was discovered that Dr Thornage's metre rule was no such thing. The one he'd purchased in the little shop in Athens was part of a faulty batch, and far from being a metre long it in fact only measured a measly ninty-nine centimetres. To the embarrassment of all concerned, the pioneering 400 metre running track at Cambridge University was only 396 metres long. The impressive times set on this – and indeed other diminutive running tracks – sent the continent into a panic

They need not have worried. In spite of Dr Thornage's efforts, British athletes failed to bring home any gold medals from Athens. The specially built boat that was meant to be filled with them went home empty.

The short metric measure passed from the BOA to the Sportsman's Club in Pall Mall, where these days it sits in a glass case, behind the bar.

PEREGRINE WICKS

Water Polo

A military man, Peregrine Wicks rose to the rank of Lieutenant Colonel in the King's Mounted Cambridgeshire Rifles – according to regimental legend the very same 'King's Horses' who failed to put Humpty Dumpty back together again in the nursery rhyme. After leaving the regiment in 1894, Wicks devoted his time to the breeding of thorough-bred horses, his great passion in life. By the turn of the century he'd achieved a modicum of success, not to mention notoriety. His piebald filly, Broom Handle, had won the St Leger, while the following year Gastropod, an outside hope for the Derby, had trodden on the Queen's foot at Epsom. She was reported to be unamused.

In addition to his horses, Wicks also had a string of polo ponies, and his team, the Newmarket Chargers, was considered one of the finest in the land. There was certainly no mistaking Lieutenant Colonel Wicks's team, with their smart red and blue outfits, and a badge in the shape of a cracked egg. Sadly, after February 1900, the team never competed again. The Lieutenant Colonel, always keen to do his duty for his country, had offered his assistance in the forthcoming Olympic Games. His contribution to the British Olympic effort came on twenty-second February, when he drowned six chestnut ponies in a private swimming pool following a misunderstanding over the requirements of water polo.

NANCY GILES

Swimming

It was in 1968 that commentator David Coleman so memorably shrieked the words: 'David Hemery wins for Britain. Who cares who finished third? It doesn't matter.' Well, it mattered to fellow Brit Robbie Brightwell whose unexpected bronze medal received scant recognition. But 1968 wasn't the first time the 'who cares' line had been uttered at the Olympic Games. Some twelve years earlier, in the 1956 Melbourne Olympics, it was a British swimmer's achievements that passed the public by.

The unlucky individual on that occasion was Nancy Giles, a sofa-stuffer with a firm of Derbyshire upholsterers, who won a gallant silver medal in the women's 200 Metres Individual Medley. She was cruelly touched out for the gold medal by the home-town favourite, Jenny Price, in a fingertip finish amidst scenes of wild jubilation. 'Jenny Price has won another bloomin' gold medal for Australia,' yelled the local commentator. 'Who cares who finished second? It might be the Pommie sheila in lane three, but I couldn't give a wombat's nadge. It's gold for Australia, and that's all that bloody well matters.'

The margin of victory, on examination of the scratchy film and primitive stopwatch, turned out to be a nail-biting three-hundredths of a second. Perhaps if Nancy Giles hadn't been such an inveterate nail-biter, the margin might have been even closer. But there could have been another reason for the British girl's narrow defeat. Unlike her Australian counterpart, who wore one of the latest cutting-edge clingy, figure-hugging swimsuits that left nothing to the imagination, Nancy Giles wore a flippy-flappy bathing dress made from wool. An experiment carried out at Keele University some twenty years later calculated that Nancy's costume more than doubled in weight when wet, and that the Derbyshire lass was hauling an extra ten pounds of woollen swimsuit as she made her way up and down the pool. The drag coefficient, the boffins calculated, probably cost Nancy Giles between ten and fifteen seconds, and had she been wearing nylon, like all the other swimmers, she would have romped home in world record time.

Her plucky silver medal should still have made the papers and given Nancy some momentary fame, but only the *Guardian* bothered to send a swimming correspondent to Melbourne, and due to an unfortunate printing error her achievements never made it into print. 'Miss J Price won the event,' began the paragraph at the bottom of page twenty-eight, 'and the silver medal was won by . . .' But the final line was missing from the finished copy, and the paper's readers never did discover who had finished in second place.

The newsreel of the women's 200 Metres Individual Medley only arrived in Britain several months later, by ship, by which time the public had forgotten all about the Melbourne Olympics and Nancy Giles.

HUGO DE VRIES

Motor Racing

Which were the first truly modern Games? Was it Athens 1896, the first to be revived in millennia? Was it London 1948, the first to be recorded in colour? Or was it Mexico 1968, the first to be broadcast via satellite? In 1956 Melbourne hosted the first games in the southern hemisphere, and made a different claim to modernity when they included a motorized sporting event in the programme.

This innovation was not without controversy. The American based 'League Against Sitting Sports', a group which had long campaigned for the removal of cycling and rowing from the Olympics, railed against the inclusion of yet another event that required no standing up at all. But the Melbourne organizers held firm, and the IOC backed them against the powerful American upright sports movement. Here was an opportunity for Australia to present a new face to the world, and show it was more than just a land filled with kangaroos, cork hats and boomerangs. Motor racing was the future – it would seize the imagination of the games.

In contrast to forward-thinking Australia, Britain in the

1950s was a drab and dreary place. Prime Minister Harold Macmillan tried to convince the nation they'd never had it so good, but there was no colour television, and no dishwashers or mangetout in the shops. Then a young motor-racing driver burst on to the scene with all the dash of a Douglas Fairbanks Junior or Douglas Fairbanks Senior, and jolted the nation out of its gloomy despondency. His name was Hugo de Vries.

Hugo de Vries, the son of Carmarthenshire's most infamous one-legged judge, had an early brush with motor sport. At the tender age of five, and egged on by irresponsible relatives, he'd ridden his Uncle Rupert's powerful Royal Enfield motorbike around the manicured family lawns, plunged through a plate-glass window and spent the next six months in traction.

A succession of ill-fated escapades, on motorbikes and in sports cars – and usually at the start of term – meant that Hugo spent more time in Kidwelly Hospital for Sick Boys than he ever did at school. But despite being pig ignorant, his father had a healthy cheque book, so it was no surprise when he went up to Oxford to study law. Within a fortnight, and after writing off a stolen coupé, he'd been sent down. Yet even within that short space of time he'd shown an aptitude for sport, earning a very hasty blue for shove ha'penny. Despite this, and an equally rare gift for bar billiards, Hugo was disinterested in pub sports. He wanted to be the first Welsh motor-racing champion of the world.

Back home in Wales, and sponging off his parents, Hugo gained a justifiable reputation for his good living. His consumption of champagne and his fondness for blondes was legendary.

In 1953, during a rare week of sobriety, Hugo went for a

trial with Peugeot, then trying to establish itself as a premier motor-racing team. Despite totalling the car on the first lap, the large cheque he'd brought with him meant he was taken on as a driver.

Two years later, having wrecked countless cars, Hugo de Vries made his debut in a Formula 1 race, at Monza. He managed to avoid crashing the car, but only because he was so drunk that he stalled it on the starting grid. Race marshals had to drag his car, complete with Hugo's comatose body, from the track, while the other drivers manoeuvred round it.

Things didn't improve at his next race. At the Nürburgring, Hugo attempted to light a cigar while the car was being filled with fuel, and two technicians were tragically consumed in the resulting fireball.

By this time Hugo was developing a worrying champagne dependency that could only be sated by quaffing large quantities of vintage bubbly. In preparation for the 1955 season he had a champagne bucket welded to the chassis of his car. This worked wonderfully, until some Veuve Clicquot leaked into the oil filter at the start of the Monaco Grand Prix, and the car never left the starting grid.

By the end of the year, Hugo de Vries's private life was very much public property. During the summer he'd dated not only the current but the previous Miss Sweden. Amiable, rich and handsome, the newspapers and magazines were full of lurid stories about him, and what's more most of them were true.

In the spring of 1955 the Melbourne Organising Committee for the Olympic Games announced they would be holding a motor-racing event. Each nation would be allowed only one competitor. There were more qualified drivers than Hugo de Vries in Britain – rather a lot, in fact – but none were as independently wealthy, and he was selected for the team.

The race itself was beset with all manner of problems. Dithering officials had neglected to bring any starting flags. They tried to make do by ripping up a red gingham tablecloth and flapping it about, but the Olympic officials insisted they would have to use a proper black and white chequered flag. It was a Sunday, however, which meant that all the shops were shut, and it was several hours before a flag was located in a motoring museum. During this lengthy delay, one of the pretty pit girls had fainted with the heat, and several drivers – including Hugo – had rushed over to administer mouth-to-mouth resuscitation. In the ensuing melée a French driver lost several teeth, the Austrian entrant was knocked unconscious and Hugo de Vries was badly concussed. It took a bottle of Ambonnay Grand Cru '48 before he was considered fit enough to drive.

By this time, though, the race was several hours late. The competition had originally been scheduled for the morning – not just to prevent any of the drivers from drinking, but also to minimize the effects of the harsh Australian sun. By three o'clock in the afternoon it was too late for that. The track, which was one of Australia's first ever tarmac roads, had turned into a molten black ribbon. Driving was impossible, although that didn't prevent the German ace, Dieter von Schleck, from trying. He made it as far as the first chicane before his expensive car churned to a halt. A relatively sober Hugo de Vries stayed rooted to the front row of the grid. The starting officials waved their flags, and the race was abandoned. The following day brought no respite from the weather, and with the track unusable, the cars ruined and most of the drivers drunk, race officials took the only sensible course of action and scrapped the event altogether.

Bitterly frustrated, Hugo returned to England where he hoped to resume his career. But before he could, tragedy struck.

On a trip to the famous herb gardens at Droitwich Castle, Hugo somehow lost control of his Maserati. The car ploughed through a row of beehives, causing mayhem in the castle grounds and sadly claiming the life of a hyper-allergic Scotsman. Hugo, who'd taken the precaution of keeping all the windows shut, escaped both injury and bee stings.

It proved to be one of Hugo de Vries's last contributions to public life. Shortly afterwards it's believed he left for France and joined the Rheims-based Brotherhood of St Mario, a religious order dedicated to achieving heaven on earth through the copious consumption of fine sparkling wines. Whether Hugo ever achieved this is anybody's guess.

'BOY X'

Discus

The story of the athlete known only by the crude appellation 'Boy X' is one of the most moving in all Olympic history, British or otherwise. It is a wretched tale that deserves to be better known.

A native of the Derbyshire Peak District he is to date the only bona fide caveman to have represented Great Britain at the Olympic Games. Yet although his story is one of unexpected and astounding gifts flowering in the most unlikely surroundings, it is not one with a happy ending.

'Boy X' – his true name was never established – was a member of the Wollangeanengenenengong people, a group of Neanderthal-like individuals who clung on among the rocks and caves of Derbyshire. Few people then had heard of the tribe's name, and even fewer were able to spell it. Seldom seen and shunned by most local people the Wollangeanengenenengong eked out a precarious existence, subsisting largely on bilberries, rabbits, wild birds and picnic leftovers during the brief summer months. Ham sandwiches were said to be a particular favourite.

It was Nicholas St Aubyn, a freelance stove designer and

FORGOTTEN SPORTING HEROES No. 14

BOY 'X'
DISCUS

botanist who first made contact with 'Boy X' in the summer of 1950. He'd parked his bull-nosed Morris in a lay-by in preparation for an afternoon wading among the peat bogs when he found himself surrounded by a group of savages, shouting and grunting and making threatening gestures. Casting aside the creeping sedges he'd gathered, St Aubyn rushed back to the safety of his car while rocks and assorted missiles rained down upon him. But as his key fumbled in the lock, one of the hairy barbarians caught Nicholas St Aubyn's eye. In his autobiography, *Training the Ape Man of Glossop,* he described at length how one of the brutes was throwing hardened cowpats rather than stones or clods of earth. Moreover, this particular youth employed a rudimentary discus technique, twisting his body on its axis before hurling the cowpat a considerable distance. As he drove away in his dented motor car, St Aubyn calculated that some cowpats had travelled over fifty yards.

In addition to his other interests Nick St Aubyn was also a keen sportsman and part time PE teacher at High Peak school, and he spoke to the headmaster about the cowpat-flinging savage. It might just be possible, he told the head, to train the hirsute teenager to throw the discus for the school. Derbyshire schools had a dismal record in the technical athletic events, most especially the discus, and the headmaster was only too eager to give the plan a try. So the pair of them took to the moors the following week armed with some ham sandwiches and Bakewell tart as bait, and a huge drift net with which to trap their victim. It worked perfectly, and soon the young savage had been brought back to the school.

Promising athlete he might be, but Nicholas St Aubyn found it impossible to communicate with the savage he dubbed 'Boy X'. The near-Neanderthal spoke no English, only a few guttural grunts, and to begin with sat crouching in the playground baring his gums to all-comers, and resolutely refusing to throw the discus. But eventually the PE teacher made a breakthrough – smearing mustard on the ham sandwiches and leaving macaroons for afters – and by sports day discuses as well as cowpats were flying from the primitive hand of 'Boy X'.

On fourteenth June, and with a school badge pinned crudely to his deerskin loincloth, 'Boy X' was presented at the Derbyshire inter-schools athletics championships. The lady mayoress of Ashbourne, who was guest of honour at the event, is reputed to have fainted at the sight of him. There were raised eyebrows at such a hairy and semi-naked boy taking part in the games, but a quick scan through the rulebook showed that nothing was out of order and 'Boy X' was allowed to compete. He won effortlessly and broke the county record, causing only a minor incident when he ate the laurel wreath presented to the victor ludorum. As impressive as the boy's feats had been, Nicholas St Aubyn knew his protégé was better than that. Later that year he entered the savage for the Amateur Athletics Championships at White City, where the athletics officials took one look at 'Boy X' and duly struck him from the list.

Undaunted, St Aubyn tried again the following year, pointing out that there was nothing in the championship's rules to prevent a caveman from competing, and his persuasive argument won the day. Next day, 'Boy X' flung the two-kilogramme discus beyond fifty-one metres, and smashed not only the British but the Commonwealth record. The athletics world would have to take notice now, especially with an Olympics approaching the following year.

There were plans to go back to the Peak District for some high altitude training, but these had to be shelved when Nicholas St Aubyn was called away on business. He was summoned to Indonesia to design a stove for President Sukarno, and left in a hurry without any thought for the welfare of 'Boy X'. Robbed of his protector, the hairy young brute was kidnapped by members of the Derbyshire Primitive Society and presented as an exhibit at the Festival of Britain, alongside the world's largest jar of lemon curd.

Ill-suited to a life which involved standing on a plinth all day and having strangers gawp at him, 'Boy X' twice attempted to run away. The oppressive concrete jungle of London's South Bank offered no shelter, however, and on both occasions the young Derbyshire caveman was ruthlessly hunted down by the Festival's security guards and returned to the exhibition.

It was a sorry-looking 'Boy X' that greeted Nicholas St Aubyn when he returned to England in early 1952. The once proud savage had been reduced to a skeletal figure. Unaware of the peculiarities of his diet, and unable to interpret his grunting, his keepers had fed him on leftovers from the Festival canteen. It was not to his liking. Chips, sausage rolls and bacon were left uneaten in his cage, as was the lemon curd – then, as now, an acquired taste.

But the intervening months had not been kind to Nicholas St Aubyn either. President Sukarno was unimpressed with the design for his new stove, and the Briton had been flung into prison. Only an intervention by the Aga Khan – a man unconnected with stoves despite his name – secured the part-time PE teacher's release. St Aubyn was shocked when he finally reached Britain and saw what had happened to his protégé. Their reunion was emotional and the pair talked for many hours into the night. Well, St Aubyn talked. 'Boy X' mostly grunted, as he gorged himself on a huge pile of ham sandwiches.

The next day the pair returned to Derbyshire to continue training, in preparation for the forthcoming Helsinki Olympics, and the savage soon began recording some prodigious distances. News of them soon reached London, and it wasn't long before the Amateur Athletic Association sent a letter to St Aubyn barring 'Boy X' from the team. Cavemen, no matter how gifted, were not welcome in a UK vest, they informed him. St Aubyn replied with a letter of his own. There were no rules preventing cavemen from competing, he contended. The only individuals who could not represent Britain at the Olympics were criminals, lunatics and cannibals, and no one could prove that 'Boy X' was any of those things. Furthermore, he pointed out, the standard in the men's discus was not especially high, and with the right sort of training, the hairy youngster might stand a chance of winning a medal in the event – something no British athlete had ever done. Convinced of these arguments or not, the Amateur Athletic Association finally agreed to let 'Boy X' compete – but insisted that he must wear a team vest. The usual practice of shaving a competition number in his back hair would no longer be permissible.

As it turned out, Nicholas St Aubyn was correct in his assessment of the discus. Consolini, the reigning champion, was in wretched form, while Gordien, the world record holder, had failed to get close to the 56.97 metre mark he'd set the summer before. It looked increasingly possible that the most unlikely member of the British team just might get himself amongst the medals.

And so, Britain's first caveman athlete headed off for the

Olympic Games. The costumiers somehow managed to find him a blazer and slacks – although no one could persuade him to put them on – and in the end it was felt that 'Boy X' might be better off sitting out the opening ceremony. UK officials were embarrassed by him. He'd bared his gums to the Duchess of Kent, and there was no guarantee that he wouldn't do something inappropriate and upset the Finnish crowd. Instead the Derbyshire caveman was kept under wraps until the discus competition finally started. But if the crowd was shocked at seeing a knuckle-dragging primitive wearing a British team vest, they didn't show it. Instead, like civilized Europeans, they concentrated on his impressive discus technique, and applauded warmly. 'Boy X' in turn responded, and he qualified comfortably for the final, behind Dillion, the American, and a resurgent Consolini. Nicholas St Aubyn, not to mention the officials from the British team, crossed their fingers for the hirsute young Derbyshire thrower.

But two days can be a long time in athletics, and something happened during that agonizing forty-eight-hour wait. Tragically for 'Boy X', they ran out of ham sandwiches in the Olympic village canteen. St Aubyn rushed to the village when he heard about this misfortune, but the games had coincided with a butcher's strike in Helsinki and ham was like gold dust – impossible to find. Desperately the freelance stove designer tried to ply the cave-boy with cheese and chutney sandwiches – but whether it was the unfamiliar Finnish bread or the tangy chutney, 'Boy X' turned his flattened nose up at it. Deprived of his natural diet, and weak from hunger, 'Boy X' finished in ninth place some four metres below his best. It was a sad but somehow inevitable conclusion to his Olympic career.

'Boy X' returned to the moors of Derbyshire as soon as he got back from Finland, but it was not a happy home-coming. Most of the Wollangeanengenenengong people had succumbed to a strain of Leicestershire flu, and it is believed that 'Boy X' himself contracted it shortly after he arrived. There were no confirmed sightings of the Wollangeanengenenengong after about 1958. It's possible that one or two of them might somehow have avoided the epidemic, but whether any of them have survived to the present day, that is surely stretching credibility.

Even though he failed to bring home a medal, 'Boy X' did have a lasting effect on the Olympic movement and the Amateur Athletic Association. After the 1952 games both bodies amended their rules to disqualify savages, Neanderthals, Cro-Magnons and Piltdown men from competing at any future Olympics. Even the revelation in 1953 that the Piltdown Man was an elaborate fraud did not cause them to further rewrite the rules of eligibility. If he were still alive and had any thoughts on the matter, 'Boy X' kept his guttural grunts to himself.

BILL REDFEARN

Fencing

These days a sporting footnote, in the 1920s Dr William Redfearn was an eminent scientist, best known for his experiments involving cats. 1923's 'Tiddles Hypothesis' is still the benchmark for Quantum Dynamics, while his 'Mr Binky Theorem' of 1925 established that it was possible to illuminate a ten-watt light bulb using only the heat from a cat-warmed cushion.

What are less well documented are Dr Redfearn's exploits in the field of Olympic fencing, and are overdue a second consideration.

As one of Britain's most eminent fencers, Bill Redfearn represented Britain not once but twice at the Olympics. His speciality was the épée, and at the 1924 Games he came within a well-oiled whisker of defeating Charles Delporte, the suave Belgian who eventually carried off the gold medal. Dr Redfearn finished in a creditable fourth place, agonizingly close to a medal, but nevertheless Britain's best ever placing in an Olympic fencing event.

Four years later, taking a well-earned break from cat-based scientific inventions, Bill Redfearn pitched up in

Amsterdam with his trusty épée in hand and gunning for the gold.

True to form he cut a swathe through the opposition, despatching one swordsman after another and reaching the semi-finals with something to spare. There he faced Marcel Chabrot, a wily Frenchman with a flashing blade and an equally impressive moustache. It was common knowledge among the fencing fraternity that Chabrot did not possess Bill Redfearn's natural skill with the épée – but what he lacked in technique the Frenchman more than made up for with Gallic guile. Chabrot had made a habit of studying his opponents – a rare trait in 1928 – and was fully aware of the British fencer's weakness for cats. Whether it was he who ordered the release of an especially attractive tabby midway through their tense bout no one will ever know, but the effect of its arrival was devastating. Chuckles broke out amongst the spectators, including the hardened fencing aficionados, as the cat seated itself on the edge of the stage and began washing itself behind its ears. In no time at all, his concentration shot, Bill Redfearn was a beaten man. His crack at the Olympic gold had gone.

No sooner had the bout finished than the British team lodged a protest, but it was rejected on the grounds that there was nothing within the sport's rules which precluded a cat from the arena. The rulebook might prohibit dogs, budgerigars, pigs, newts, lampreys and rabbits, but it said nothing about cats, and that was that.

Bill Redfearn failed to turn up for his bronze medal play-off the following day and was thus placed fourth for the second Games in succession. It later emerged that rather than compete he'd gone instead to Amsterdam's famous

Cat Market to console himself, buying a short-haired tortoiseshell he named Gaston.

Bill Redfearn never competed at another Olympic Games, instead devoting the rest of his life to the pursuit of science and the love of cats – usually both at the same time. In 1931 he published 'Gaston's Principle' (subsequently disproved) and in 1940, while the country was under siege at the Battle of Britain, he completed his three-year study into the efficiency of cats' tongues. His 'Quiller Memorandum' (which should not be confused with the film of the same name) produced the classic formula $3x + 2(y + 43)$ where y is the cat's tongue and x is a saucer of carnation milk, which established exactly how the roughness of a cat's tongue increased the efficiency of its licking.

Dr Bill Redfearn's final legacy was the 'Smokey Theorem', which took its name from one of his favourite cats and was to prove his undoing. In trying to administer a worming tablet the former Olympic fencer chased after the animal, which had strayed on to a nearby railway line. A few minutes later Dr Redfearn proved his theory – otherwise untitled – that a human being cannot withstand the impact of a steam-powered locomotive travelling at ninety miles an hour.

ERNEST COATES

Gymnastics

One of the more controversial – some might say shameful – episodes in British Olympic history took place at the Los Angeles Games of 1932. Such was its infamy that the whole affair was subsequently hushed up – a most ironic turn of events in view of what had happened.

The man at the centre of this sporting storm was Ernest Coates, long forgotten now but something of a minor celebrity in the late 1920s. A factory worker from Rossendale in Lancashire, Ernest was renowned for the quality of his cough. It had a full-bodied liquid quality with wheezing after notes, and had won him several rosettes in Lancashire shows. By 1930 his fame and cough had spread beyond the north-west thanks to his unexpected triumph in Antwerp's prestigious Phlegmiade. The Phlegmiade was the pinnacle of competitive coughing, and the Belgian judges were notoriously reluctant to reward a foreign cough. Ernest Coates won them round. His debilitating but lyrical hack impressed all who heard it and won him both a commendation and a splendid silver salver. It was to prove a defining moment both for Ernest Coates and for British sport.

The 1920s, of course, was the golden age of the great British cough. A century of heavy industrialization, combined with poor healthcare and a chain-smoking culture meant that the domestic lung had never been less healthy. Yet for some of the lucky ones, gifted enough to win talent shows or hacking competitions, a decent cough could mean a way out of poverty.

Ernest Coates' distinctive bark attracted a good degree of publicity and reached the influential ears of the head of British gymnastics, Colonel H.H. 'H.' Meredith. The colonel told the wheezing Lancastrian that he possessed a singular talent that could assist his gymnasts. It was time his impressive cough was put at the service of the nation. Little Annie Weaver and Madge Honeycutt were both considered promising young gymnasts, perhaps with a chance of a minor medal in the women's competition. A bronze or even a silver was a possibility, although conventional wisdom had it that the young Swede, Jutte Lindholm, was close to unbeatable. The only chink in Miss Lindholm's armour, the colonel explained, was her brittle concentration. It was certainly fragile enough that a handily placed cough during one of the more difficult moments of her routine would disturb her concentration. You could sit at the back of the gymnastics arena, Meredith said, and bellow your lungs out. After that she'd be bound to miss a vault, stagger off a beam or fail to land one of her tumbles properly. Plied with cigarettes and hard cash and yet more cigarettes, Ernest Coates eventually agreed. His only concern, that by receiving payment for coughing he'd be rendered ineligible to compete in future Olympics, was brushed aside by Colonel Meredith. Coughing would never be part of the Olympic programme, he insisted haughtily.

To sustain his medal-winning cough, Coates was sent off for damp weather training. This meant spending six months in his native Rossendale smoking eighty cigarettes a day. The regime suited him well, and by the time he reached Los Angeles in the summer of 1932, Ernest Coates had a ripe, ear-splitting cough. But no sooner had the Lancastrian arrived in the States than his problems began. The supply of cigarettes which constituted his luggage was impounded by the US Customs Agency, and Ernest discovered that his brand of choice, Black Cat untipped, was unavailable in America. The worried British team tried the Embassy and the Consulate, but they couldn't provide any cigarettes either. Coates tried adapting to the home-grown cigarettes, but found them an unsatisfactory smoke, which did nothing for his cough. Worse was to follow.

The California Dome, venue to the gymnastics events, was declared a smoke-free zone, perhaps the first in world history. At the previous games, the gymnastics events had taken place in a fug of cigarette smoke, and some of the judges had complained of being unable to see properly.

So it was a dispirited Ernest Coates who took his place in the Dome. Deprived of his precious cigarettes, he sat down to watch five hours of gymnastics – a sport that didn't interest him in the slightest. Smoke free it might have been, but the over-zealous Californians, in their effort to clean up the spanking new arena, had caused clouds of dust. Even before any of the gymnasts had competed, poor Ernest Coates had a coughing fit, collapsed breathlessly on the floor and was escorted from the Dome. When the competition finally took place the British gymnasts performed brilliantly, winning silver and bronze behind the Italian girl,

Paola Negrini. As for Jutte Lindholm, she missed the event completely, with a bad cough.

It turned out that Colonel Meredith was wrong about coughing in the Olympics. In early 1935 Germany announced that Teutonic and Non-Teutonic Coughing were both to be included as demonstration events at the 1936 Berlin Games. They were obvious choices. Following the war Germany still had thousands of mustard-gas sufferers to choose from, so they quite fancied their chances of winning.

It was, of course, doubly too late for Ernest Coates. As a professional cougher he would have been ineligible to compete – but more unfortunately, and crucially, he was dead. He caught a chill in the winter of 1934 and died after a short, loud illness.

Not that he'd have missed anything. Neither coughing event turned out to be a success and the 1936 Olympics proved to be the death rattle for the competitive cough.

VICE-ADMIRAL SIR WILLIAM BARNETT AND OTHERS

Dreadnought Racing

Anyone who doubts that the First World War was a conflict waiting to happen need only look at the programme for the 1912 Olympics to convince themselves otherwise. In addition to the customary medals for athletics, swimming, wrestling and so forth, no less than twenty-four gold medals were awarded for sailing. Of these, a mere five events involved conventional wooden yachts. The remaining nineteen were between assorted classes of warships. It's an episode rarely discussed nowadays, but one which brought the Olympic movement perilously close to financial ruin.

From our vantage point, in the early twenty-first century, it's hard to imagine the host nation, Sweden, a country admired for its sense of fair play and its ability to steer clear of global conflicts, staging races between fully armed warships. But the suggestion that the Olympic Games was an appropriate venue for racing battleships did not come from the Swedes. It was all the idea of the Germans and the British.

By 1912, both countries had built dozens and dozens of

warships and desired, quite innocently, to test their fleet's capability. Might it not be possible, they asked, to have a review in the Gulf of Bothnia? The Swedes reluctantly agreed and, after much diplomatic to-ing and fro-ing, consented to a race around the lighthouse and back in Stockholm harbour between one German and one British ship. The Swedes were quite firm about it. One ship each; absolutely no fleets; end of story. They might have got their way had it not been for the Germans spotting that the British ship, HMS *Redoubtable*, possessed more aft guns than their own SMS *Gewaltig*. The next day the slightly larger SMS *Unerschütterlich* arrived in Stockholm. The British, understandably piqued at this display of one-upmanship by the Germans, and not wishing them to think they had sent their biggest ship, replied with HMS *Imperturbable*. It was an impressive warship – just a little big bigger than the German vessel. Another two days passed before the German Navy, having spotted that the latest British ship was just a teensy weensy bit bigger than their last one, duly responded with the enormous SMS *Riesengross*. A month after that – having first consulted the tape measure – Britain cancelled HMS *Unsinkable*'s duties in the South Atlantic and sent it to Sweden, under the command of Vice-Admiral Sir William Barnett. The Germans subsequently despatched another ship, SMS *Unversenkbar*, which was again bettered by the British, and which in turn was countered by another German battleship. By the time the Olympic Games started, in May 1912, Stockholm harbour was choked with a vast flotilla of battle cruisers, gunboats, dreadnoughts and submarines.

There was every chance, with so many munitions-laden ships around, that full blown hostilities might break out. A party, held to celebrate Midshipman Herbert 'Guppy' Shanklin's thirtieth birthday, almost turned to disaster when some rockets, fired from the deck of HMS *Incorrigible*, fizzed too close to one of the German ships. Flags were raised, ambassadors were withdrawn and, as both nations briefly rattled maritime sabres, Europe stood on the brink of war. The tension was only defused when German High Command supplied SMS *Unversenkbar* with some retaliatory Roman candles. The Stockholm organizers therefore hastily arranged no less than nineteen new events, pairing off the ships and submarines as best they could to ensure fair play. All this dragged on throughout the summer and autumn of 1912, long after the rest of the games had packed up and left Sweden.

For the record, British warships won ten events to the Germans' nine, and while the big guns weren't actually fired – except in celebration at the finish line – the dreadnought races had profound consequences for the future of the Olympic movement, and indeed the world in general. The handing out of approximately 1,700 gold and 1,700 silver medals after every contest almost bankrupted the Olympics; it ought to be remembered that in those days the medals were solid gold and silver. The medal ceremonies dragged on interminably, day after day, as one sailor after another clambered on to the podium. The Duchess of Kalmar fainted twice whilst handing out medals, and in later life attributed the muscle strain in her forearm to a repetitive injury caused hanging medals round sailors' necks.

Despite the fact that neither fleet fired a shot in anger, the dreadnought races did not pass off entirely without incident. The Tornado yachting class, in which the Swedes had high hopes of a medal themselves, had to be abandoned when HMS *Incorrigible*, under the command of Admiral E.G. Spencer, ploughed through the boats and turned them into matchsticks.

British naval personnel collected over 13,000 gold medals during the 1912 Stockholm games – Stoker Jim Robbins, the armed forces coal-shovelling champion, picked up no fewer than five, having been transferred from ship to ship as his shovelling services were required.

The slender loss – by ten races to nine – was received very badly by German naval command. The Kaiser, hopping mad, ordered that dozens more warships be built and began looking for vacant dates in his diary when a rematch could be arranged with the British Navy. It came sooner than anyone expected.

Most of the warships from the Stockholm Olympics – both German and British – saw active service in the First World War, and many gallant gold and silver medallists from both sides lost their lives. It's sad to report that Vice-Admiral Sir William Barnett was one of them. He perished at the Battle of Jutland in 1916, when HMS *Unsinkable* failed to live up to her name. He went down with his ship, along with more than 1,300 gold medallists.

RON DRIFFIELD

Javelin

Lower Yateby in Lincolnshire is largely famous for three things. The first is the Lower Yateby Viaduct, which contains one of the most enormous spans of Lincolnshire brick to be found anywhere, built by Sir Edwin Spooner in 1788. The second is the Lower Yateby Treasure, a horde of Anglo-Saxon jewels and trinkets discovered as the viaduct was being built, and which ended up in Sir Edwin Spooner's house. The third and most recent reason for Lower Yateby's fame is the Lower Yateby Canal Boat Murders – gruesome killings which were carried out on the viaduct close to the spot where the treasure was found. That the village was also the home of Ron Driffield, Britain's premier exponent of the javelin in the late 1950s, is a fact the people of Lower Yateby – and most of Great Britain – have chosen to forget.

Ronald Wesley Driffield was born in Lincolnshire in 1930. His parents, Ronald senior and Mavis, both churchgoers and keen amateur dramatists, ran the local sub-post office. Ronald, the youngest of three children, grew up in the shadow of the viaduct, and from an early age played games of strength with his friends, shinning up ropes which dangled from the cavernous arches. Like many of his contemporaries, Ron suffered from the affliction known as Lincolnshire Arm, an uncommon ailment these days, but widespread in the early 1940s. The sufferer typically has one limb more noticeably developed than the other – usually the right one. Schoolboys with muscular right arms were something of an embarrassment amongst the prurient folk of 1940s Lincolnshire and Ron, like the other boys, was encouraged to take up a pursuit that would keep his right arm healthily occupied. Some boys were directed towards digging potatoes or sawing wood; Ron Driffield took up the javelin.

Lincolnshire, for many years the laughing stock of youth athletics, had been steadily improving in school sports during the previous decade, and the addition of Ron, a javelin natural, tipped the balance in their favour. Spearheaded – ironically – by Ron Driffield, the county not only won the national javelin championships but also beat Cambridgeshire at tiddlywinks and Cumberland and Westmoreland at fell running. It was a seismic result which sent shock waves through the world of 1940s school sports, and put Lincolnshire – not renowned as a hot bed of either javelin throwing or scrambling up hillsides – on the map. The climax came in June 1945 when the county was crowned British junior athletics champion. The defeat of Nazi Germany that same month made Lincolnshire doubly proud.

In his teenage years, Ron, an impressionable young man, came under the sway of Brother Bernard, a local poultry and potato farmer and sometime mystic, who'd been wandering Lincolnshire preaching a simple message. Live simply, said Brother Bernard, whilst also mentioning that his followers should give all their worldly goods to him and eat only a strict lactosolanarian diet – that is, nothing but egg and chips. Ron Driffield took Brother Bernard at his word, much to the consternation of his mother. Rationing was still in force in 1948, and black-market eggs and potatoes could be very expensive – especially when they were bought from Brother Bernard's farm. Mrs Driffield told her son not to be so stupid and eat a proper diet but, like most teenage boys before or since, Ron ignored his mother. In fact, he went further, told her where she could stick it, and left home.

As well as being an age of food shortages, the 1940s was a blunt decade. Cars had rounded shapes; chairs were dumpy; television sets didn't have corners; hairstyles were curly; while Britain's top spy was the tellingly named Anthony Blunt. It was the same in the world of sport, where javelins had stubby rounded tips that didn't stick into the ground properly. As a consequence, British javelin throwing was in something of a crisis. Most of the country's metal had been requisitioned during the war to build aeroplanes and ships, and there was almost nothing left over to put on the tips of javelins. The British all-wooden javelin was an aerodynamic disaster. To the surprise of no one, Sweden, a nation which had skipped the Second World War and which had its own steel supply, had become the powerhouse of men's javelin. At the London Olympics of 1948, an eighteen-year-old Ron Driffield watched transfixed from the stands as the Swede Magnus Hedblom won the gold medal. So transfixed, in fact, that he let his egg and chips go cold.

Using a home-made zinc-tipped javelin Ron Driffield won the East of England championships in the summer of 1940. Not long afterwards Ron met a local girl, Marjorie Miller, and following an ardent display of wooing – mainly at

Stamford's top transport café – she finally consented to marry him. If Marjorie felt any sense of anti-climax at the 50 plates of egg and chips at their wedding reception, she hid her disappointment well.

Married life suited Ron. In March 1954 Marjorie gave birth to a daughter, Bernardette, and a few months later the Lower Yateby man won an unexpected silver medal at the Commonwealth Games in Canada. Alas, he was unable to build on his success straightaway. In the spring of 1955 he cut his right hand with a potato peeler and missed the entire season.

During his injury lay off, Ron employed a local blacksmith, Walter Phillips, to sharpen his javelins for him. It worked a treat, and at an athletics meeting in Leeds he smashed the British record. But triumph soon turned to tragedy for the Lincolnshire thrower. Athletics officials deemed that the sharpening had reduced the weight of the javelin, and Ron Driffield's throw was scrubbed from the record books. His attempt to regain it the following weekend at Crystal Palace with a sharp – and legal – javelin came to nothing. On the Friday Ron scalded his hand with some boiling chip fat and he had to sit out the remainder of the season.

His mood in the meantime wasn't improved by news of the untimely death of Brother Bernard. The Sage of the Wolds had been killed when his helicopter had crashed into the roof of his sixty-bedroom mansion. A man who normally kept his emotions in check, Ron Driffield was seen to shed a tear at Brother Bernard's funeral as the poultry-and-potato-farmer-turned-mystic's solid gold coffin was lowered into the loamy Lincolnshire soil.

Ron Driffield's javelin comeback was hampered by bouts of ill health. Salmonella came hard on the heels of constipation, which in turn was followed by a wasting complaint. The terrible potato shortage of 1958 didn't help matters. Weak and out of sorts, Ron could barely grip a javelin, let alone throw one. His pitiful display at the Amateur Athletics Championships that year led seasoned javelin experts to declare that the Lower Yateby man's best days were behind him. How wrong they were.

In late 1959, Ron Driffield made his long-awaited comeback at the Egg Marketing Board Athletics Classic, thanks in no small part to a bumper crop of early Kerr's Pinks. The distinctive Irish spud became the vegetable craze of the New Year. Some even dubbed it the 'Rock 'n' Roll Potato' when Eddie Cochran sang about its merits on *Six-Five Special* in his song 'Do the Mash':

> I love my Maris Pipers
> And Russet Burbanks too
> A Jersey Royal you can fry or boil
> That's what I'm tellin' you.
>
> But there's one kinda tater
> You can cook up in a wink
> You can boil or bake, have as chips with steak
> And they call those babies Kerr's Pinks.
>
> You do the mash, mash, mash
> You do the mash, mash, mash
> You do the mash, you do the mash
> You do the m-a-a-a-ash!

Tragically Eddie's untimely death on the A4 the next week robbed the world of a major singing talent, and 'Do The

Mash' was never released. Not that Ron Driffield paid much attention. No lover of music, he was far more interested in the Kerr's Pinks, which while predominantly a mashing potato did also make excellent chips.

Refortified and with the Olympics in Rome to look forward to later that year, Ron began flinging the javelin for all he was worth, despite the cumbersome bandages that wrapped his hand. He achieved some prodigious distances, and despite an untimely injury with a crinkle cutter – fortunately only to his left hand – Ron Driffield was selected for the British Olympic team. As he marched behind the British flag the Lincolnshire thrower was easily recognizable to athletics fans – his pallid skin and appalling complexion made him unmistakable.

The Olympic javelin final, as it turned out, was an anti-climax. The Soviet Viktor Tsibulenko unleashed a throw of 84.64 metres in the first round, and none of the other competitors came anywhere near it. Ron Driffield finished a tantalizing fourth – just twenty centimetres from a bronze medal – and, with a throw of 78.40 metres, was well below his best.

Inevitably, questions were asked, and not just in the faddy diet press. Why had he insisted on cooking his own egg and chips? How had he managed to burn his hand on the gas ring? Or had the cooking oil got on to his fingers and prevented him from gripping the javelin properly? No one had the faintest idea.

If the Lincolnshire lactosolanarian thought the worst was behind him he was bitterly mistaken. He returned to Lower Yateby to discover that Marjorie had been having a torrid affair with Walter Phillips, Ron's one time javelin sharpener, and that the pair had moved into an egg-free love nest. An angry Ron finally tracked them down, but while he was distracted by some unusual potatoes he'd spotted in the kitchen, the lovers fled. Ron gave chase and watched in frustration as Walter and Marjorie made their escape by canal boat. Channelling his fury, as he stood beneath the Lower Yateby Viaduct Ron Driffield launched one of his sharpest javelins. It sailed through the air, went through one of the gaily painted barge windows and straight through the two lovers, killing them at once. It was a grisly scene, but an impressive throw nonetheless. At a shade under eighty-one metres it would have won Ron Driffield an Olympic silver medal had he done it in Rome. He was arrested the same night, sobbing uncontrollably as he fried his eggs.

Lincolnshire, like the rest of Britain, still retained the death penalty in 1960 and it was fully expected that the Lower Yateby man would hang for his crime. It never came to pass. While on remand in Louth Prison Ron Driffield was killed by a fellow inmate, stabbed to death with a fork during an argument over the merits of the Jersey Royal.

Ron Driffield was cremated and his ashes were sprinkled over a potato field just outside Lower Yateby.

TOM DRAKE

Dressage

There aren't many British sportsmen who can claim to have pranced their way out of the ghetto. But Tom Drake, the so-called 'Wild Man of Dressage', was one such individual. A genuine contender for a gold medal at the 1988 Games in Korea, the whole country should by rights have been perched on the edge of their sofas watching him bob up and down and up and down – and occasionally across and back – the dressage arena. But his moment in the sporting spotlight did not materialize. For reasons completely beyond Tom Drake's control there were no cameras at the dressage arena, so the British public never saw what turned out to be one of the most calamitous performances by a British Olympian. After being quietly forgotten for more than twenty years, it's time the story was retold.

Tom Drake was born in the East End of London in the summer of 1964, as luck would have it during the only previous occasion the Olympics had been held in Asia. He was technically a Cockney, born within the sound of Bow Bells, although as Tom was somewhat hard of hearing whether he could technically have heard the bells or not has

been fiercely debated by a number of Cockney historians. The Pearly Professor of Social 'Istory, 'Dr' Bert Brownin', gives him the benefit of the doubt.

Tom's mother Betty, a keen sports fan, had gone into labour while the athletes were warming up for the men's 200 metres final, causing her to miss an otherwise undistinguished race, won by the American Henry Carr. She had great hopes for her young son, but he showed little promise – neither academically, nor in the field of sport. Instead he was disruptive, disrespectful and trouble to everyone who crossed his path. That was to change when Tom went to his secondary school, the Alderman Arthur W. Bacon Secondary Modern, in September 1975. Thanks to an ancient City of London charter, the school was the beneficiary of an unusual gift. Each academic year one of the lucky pupils received: 'breeches made from the finest Romford muslin, and a hat that do covereth the noggin foresquare'. In 1976, Tom Drake was the unexpected recipient of this well-intentioned if pointless custom, which required that pupils go to school bedecked with plumed hats or toppers, while often walking barefoot. Tom, one of the boys lucky enough to wear shoes, was presented with a splendid plush top-hat – which he loved – and some uncomfortable rough cloth trousers of which he was rather less fond.

The mid 1970s was a radical era for the ancient sport of dressage. Some people had begun questioning the idea of horse discipline as an Olympic event, and the dressage authorities, perhaps mindful of this criticism, had begun to look for ways to make the sport more relevant to the late twentieth century. The British Dressage Association, determined to rid the event of its stuffy, upper-class image, hosted an open day at Lord Nuneaton's country estate. It was a well-intentioned gesture which rather backfired, as anyone who looked slightly scruffy or who had an inner-city postcode was turned away at the gates. Embarrassed at this debacle, the breakaway British Dressage Society went on the offensive, visiting working-class schools to preach the message. By chance they paid a visit to Alderman Arthur's, where they noticed the boy in the muslin breeches and top hat. The twelve-year-old Tom was immediately offered the chance to ride one of the horses, and the young tearaway took to it like a duck – or indeed a drake – to water. He walked and trotted and trotted and walked the horse up and down the makeshift dressage arena (which was in fact nothing more than the school playground sprinkled with a little dressage dirt) like an expert.

It didn't take long for news of this grubby Cockney urchin to travel along the dressage grapevine and reach the ears of those in authority. Here was a boy who was a natural – who might be able to improve the miserable standing of British dressage. Despite some misgivings – such as the boy's impenetrable accent and his use of strong language – Tom Drake was granted a scholarship, and with his mum's blessings ringing in his less than perfect ears he was packed off to the British Dressage School in deepest Gloucestershire. Soon, thanks to the influence of his fellow trainees, Tom's accent softened – even if his language didn't – and cups and rosettes soon began to stack up on the mantelpiece of his dormitory room. Then punk happened.

The punk ethos, which was in full swing by 1978, had been slow to reach the formal world of dressage. Indeed, experienced British equestrians like Diane Peterson and Dominic Mumby had stated their objection to the loud and aggressive music with its nihilist attitude, which seemed to contradict all the niceties of horsey etiquette. Tom Drake thought otherwise. He eagerly embraced the subculture, sticking a bolt through his nose, slashing his bright red jacket and fixing it back together with safety pins, and, most contentiously of all, decorating his top hat with swear words.

In the following spring he acquired a splendid chestnut gelding, which he named Weeping Ulcer, although only after the first dozen suggestions had been rejected by the British Dressage Society. Tom Drake and Weeping Ulcer – instantly recognizable with his spiked mane – cut quite a dash on the dressage circuit, and as the trophies continued to mount up expectation grew that the pair might one day even be in with a shout at the Olympics.

The 1980 Games, held in Moscow, came a little too soon for Tom Drake, who was only sixteen years old. In any case the British equestrian team decided to boycott the event in protest at the Soviet invasion of Afghanistan, and not a single British horse went to Russia. Four years and a mountain of rosettes later, Tom Drake was eager to compete. Unfortunately, some ill-judged profanities on Terry Wogan's chat show and his insistence on wearing his swear-word covered top hat in front of the cameras scuppered his chances. He was removed from the Olympic dressage squad, which subsequently failed to win a single medal at the Games.

By the time of the Seoul Olympics in the summer of 1988, Tom Drake was twenty-four years old – a seasoned dressage rider, although still relatively young compared to his fellow competitors. He and Weeping Ulcer arrived in Korea with high hopes. According to *Hoof*, the magazine of the dressage devotee, there was no better bet for gold than the bolt-nosed Briton and his mount.

The preliminary rounds went well, and the pair qualified comfortably for the final, prancing through in first place. But thereafter the Olympic experience turned sour for Tom Drake. The Swiss equestrian team had taken exception to his customized topper and demanded that it be banned for the final. It would not do to have English swear words daubed on a top hat transmitted into countless millions of homes around the world, they argued. To Tom Drake's horror, the International Dressage Federation agreed, telling him that for the good name of the sport, he would not be allowed to wear his rude hat. An incensed Tom lost his temper, kicking over a coffee table and punching an official, breaking not only the table, but also his foot and the judge's jaw.

Only dramatic pleading by the British chef d'équipe, Mr Peters, prevented Tom Drake from quitting the games. Now was no time to make rash decisions he might regret for the rest of his life, Mr Peters explained. Britain was depending on Tom and Weeping Ulcer for dressage glory. He owed it to the folks back home to wear a conventional hat and canter his way to victory. With a heavy heart, Tom Drake agreed.

The following morning, on the day of the final, while Tom relaxed listening to the Clash, an equerry was sent out to Seoul's best millinery shop to buy a top hat. He rushed back to the dressage arena with scarcely a moment to spare and handed over the officially sanctioned headgear. No sooner was it atop the Drake head than disaster struck. Weeping Ulcer had taken no more than a few flamboyant steps into the dressage ring when the top hat slipped down over Tom's eyes, rendering him, to all intents and purposes, blind. The British rider did his best to lift it up but the top hat stuck firm, and the jerking movements caused by his attempts to remove it made Weeping Ulcer miss his footing. What should have been a straightforward trot and canter half-pass (the bit where the horse moves diagonally while keeping its body parallel to the side wall) turned into more of a pirouette, and by the time Tom had finally struggled free Weeping Ulcer was back to front and trotting when he should have been cantering. To add insult to injury, the troublesome topper slipped from Tom's grasp and it fell directly in Weeping Ulcer's path. The horse duly put his foot through it, and it lodged half-way up his ankle. His attempts to prance it off proved unsuccessful. By the time the duo finished, a couple of minutes later, the normally po-faced dressage crowd were doubled up in laughter. Tom Drake stormed back to the Olympic village where he kicked over another coffee table (with his good foot) and destroyed a fizzy drinks dispenser. It earned him a reprimand – but in truth, Tom Drake had every right to be angry.

Unbeknownst to either Tom or the British equestrian team, South Korea had not been a signatory to the International Hat Sizes Convention – their hat sizes being somewhat larger than ours – and what was bought as a size 7½ turned out to be closer to a size 9.

The British public had seen nothing of this unedifying fiasco. Just as the Cockney equestrian was about to compete, news had broken that Ben Johnson, the winner of the men's one hundred metres, had failed a drugs test. A furore erupted which quickly became the story of the 1988 Olympic Games, overshadowing everything else. Camera crews scheduled for fencing, handball and dressage were hastily packed off to Ben Johnson's shame-faced press conference, and Tom Drake's long-awaited debut in the dressage final was never filmed.

Tom's mother – an erratic presence on the dressage circuit over the preceding years – also failed to see her son's ignominious performance. On her way to Korea, she'd been involved in an unseemly row at Heathrow airport over a cab fare, and after a scuffle she was thrown into a padded cell, which meant that she missed her flight.

Tom Drake made a half-hearted bid for selection to the Barcelona games in 1992, but by then Weeping Ulcer had sashayed his last, and with insufficient time to train a new horse, he decided to call it a day.

As it turned out, dressage's loss was the sweet-eater's gain. Tom Drake ploughed his money into the butterscotch and lemon bon-bon market, and over the next few years made prodigious amounts of money from the production of quality sweets. He left the country in 2001 and lives today in Barbados, in a splendid cliff-top property with an extremely rude name.

'AMPLE' ARTHUR CARTWRIGHT

Football

In his day, the 1950s, 'Ample' Arthur Cartwright was one of the country's finest footballers. But despite representing Britain at the Olympic Games, there were those that said 'Ample' Arthur never fulfilled his potential, blighted as it was by a lifelong obsession with archaeology.

'Ample' Arthur Cartwright, or plain Arthur back then, was born in 1928 in Oldham to Charles and Enid, a couple who owned Lancashire's largest cocker spaniel. Charles Cartwright worked long hours at the local thermometer factory which turned out to be a mixed blessing, because though it put bread on the family table, the overexposure to mercury hastened him to an early grave. To make ends meet Mrs Cartwright took in washing, dabbled in prostitution and sold off almost all the family possessions, save one – a Moroccan bound volume on Roman archaeology which was young Arthur's favourite book. Unfortunately, the book helped prop up the family table, and without it the bread rolled off on to the dirty floor.

To make room for lodgers, and to stop the bread rolling off the table, Arthur was packed off to Mrs Grimshaw's

Academy. No one in the school knew more than he did about Etruscan high glaze pottery, although back in the 1930s archaeology didn't feature prominently on the curriculum of many Lancashire infants' schools. What they did specialize in was sport, and it didn't take long for young Arthur to show his talent. Football, cricket, ocean-going yachting – he was best in the school at all of them, which was an impressive statistic even allowing for the fact he was the only child in the academy not afflicted with rickets, polio and all those other terrible things. He also got extremely fat, as meals were dished out on a first-come, first-served, race-to-the-table basis.

Despite his chubbiness, as one of the few able-bodied boys in Lancashire 'Ample' Arthur Cartwright attracted the attention of several football clubs. In 1945, as the war ended, Manchester United and Liverpool – both powerful teams back then – offered him a contract as a professional footballer. He turned them both down in favour of his home town club, Oldham Athletic. As luck would have it Oldham ran their own archaeology scholarship in lieu of pay, and they promised Arthur a job in the local museum doing menial things.

Oldham's manager at the time was Jack Hedges, a no-nonsense ex-welder with a penchant for portly footballers. 'Bulky' Arthur Bradshaw, Arthur 'Big Boy' Fogarty, 'Chubby' Arthur McCandless and Arthur 'Would You Look At The Size Of Him' Livermore all made their names at the club. The only player in the team not called Arthur was centre forward Freddie 'Fat As Butter' Jones, a twenty-goal-a-season man who later went to prison for doing unspeakable things to seabirds.

In February 1946 'Ample' Arthur Cartwright almost made

his debut in a game against Middlesbrough. A buzz quickly built up at Boundary Park as the expectant Oldham crowd watched the fat lad effortlessly juggle the heavy leather football in the pre-match kick-about. Gasps duly turned to groans when a message came over the loudspeakers telling Arthur he had to go to the local museum. The club had heard a rumour that Sheffield Wednesday were sending an expedition to find the fabled lost city of Cetzoatapetl in Central America. Oldham Athletic didn't want to get left behind in the search for Aztec treasure in Mexico, so 'Ample' Arthur was packed off on an expedition with some other promising footballers to see if they could find it first. Two years later he returned, as fat as ever, with the news that he'd been unable to locate the fabled lost city. The only good news was that the Sheffield Wednesday expedition hadn't found it either. After 400 years the fabled lost city of Cetzoatapetl remained resolutely lost.

'Ample' Arthur spent the next few years in the tragic no-man's-land twixt archaeology and football. In 1951 his passion earned him a suspension when he was caught digging an eight-foot hole in the York City goalmouth, ostensibly looking for Roman pottery. All he found was a thrupenny bit, which had probably fallen from the grounds-man's pocket.

It was with a heavy heart, and a bag full of archaeological remains, that 'Ample' Arthur left his beloved Oldham Athletic in 1956. In the cash-strapped post-war era, football clubs began to concentrate exclusively on their football. Hartlepool abandoned its Butterfly Collecting Club; Manchester City closed their Gilbert and Sullivan D'Oyly Carte Theatre midway through a critically acclaimed production of *HMS Pinafore*; while in 1957 Oldham Athletic shut their archaeology museum once and for all.

Dismayed at this turn of events, 'Ample' Arthur joined the only team which still maintained some links with archaeology, Bradford City, who promptly sent him on a scholarship to Italy, run by Juventus football club. In return the Italian champions sent over a promising full-back to sift through some Anglo-Saxon burial mounds.

It didn't take Arthur long to fall in love with the country. There were rich pickings in the Italian soil, where it seemed one need only swing a pickaxe into the ground to discover a host of ancient artefacts – usually smashed to bits by the pickaxe. But it wasn't just the archaeology that captured Arthur's heart. He met a local girl, Lucia, a bright young thing with winsome eyes who worked on a farm where she strangled turkeys. Arthur's football improved meanwhile, spurred on no doubt by the girl of his dreams and a room cluttered from floor to ceiling with broken Roman pottery. He scored twelve goals in the Italian league that season, winning himself a championship medal and the nickname *'Il Grande Inglese di ceramica fracassata'* – literally, 'The Ample Englishman of the Broken Pots'.

While Arthur was hitting the headlines in the Italian league, the British football team had qualified for the Rome Olympics. A strictly amateur outfit – as the Games demanded in those days – by the time the Olympics arrived most of the players had signed professional terms, leaving only a patchwork squad. What was needed was a man who had played at the very top level, who could mould the squad and lead the team to glory, and who, most importantly of all, was an amateur. 'Ample' Arthur Cartwright was just the man. Over the years, he'd never received so much as a penny from any of the clubs he'd played for – only bits and pieces of pottery and glass in lieu of payment. Approached with an offer to join the team as player-manager, Arthur steadfastly refused. He had a collection of Byzantine slipware, he explained, that wouldn't catalogue itself. Only the offer of a complimentary pickaxe and sifting griddle persuaded him to change his mind.

As it turned out, though, 'Ample' Arthur was unable to play. On the eve of the Games he slipped a disc trying to lever an amphora out of the ground with a crowbar, and resigned himself to sitting on the bench.

The campaign – much like the Roman army's display at the Battle of Cannae in 216 BC – was little short of a disaster. The British team, only a few of whom were classically educated, failed to understand 'Ample' Arthur's tactical instructions, barked from the touchline in a Lancastrian-tinged Latin. The team suffered embarrassing defeats against Egypt and Argentina, only gaining credit in their last match when they held the eventual gold medallists, Yugoslavia, to a goalless draw. The press described the plucky British players as 'working like Trojans', which was ironic, as that was the exact formation that 'Ample' Arthur had deployed, even taking the players to the stadium in a hastily constructed wooden horse to hammer home his message.

After a final year in Italy 'Ample' Arthur Cartwright returned to Oldham with his new wife and several container loads of uncatalogued archaeological bric-a-brac. He died, largely forgotten, in 1993. His collection of ancient artefacts, which he'd spent the better part of his life amassing, was thrown into a skip by his surviving family before his body was even cold.

He did, however, leave one unusual legacy, the result of

an unusual stipulation in his will. Before burial, and at his request, 'Ample' Arthur's body was rendered into a viscous fat, which he insisted should be used as a human dubbin to rub into leather footballs and protect them from the ravages of the weather. It is believed that Oldham Athletic still possess an unopened jar of 'Ample' Arthur dubbin, perhaps the only one left remaining.

ERROL PEARCE

Cycling

It was always said of Errol Pearce that he was one of the nicest and most trusting men in British sport. As a matter of fact, he won an award for it. Unfortunately he lost it almost immediately. A man promised to fix the silver trophy on to an onyx base and Errol duly handed it over. He never saw the man, or the trophy, or his £46.50 fixing fee ever again.

Errol Stuart Pearce was born in Solihull on twenty-fourth March 1979. He was named in honour of St Errol, the patron saint of gravy and tuberculosis. His parents, originally from St Vincent in the Grenadines, were humble share-croppers, employed by the Birmingham Municipal Bank to trim the tatty edge of share certificates with special golden scissors. They dreamed of a better life for their robust young son, who was blessed with impeccable manners and a muscular pair of thighs. Such a combination pointed to only one place – the recently formed Solihull College of Etiquette and Cycling.

It didn't take long for Errol's supreme cycling ability – and generous nature – to show itself. In the Birmingham and District Under-Fifteen Cycling Championships of 1993 he stormed through to the final, where he was the over-whelming favourite. His opponent, Jeremy Fingest, had qualified with a much slower time. But what Fingest lacked in basic speed he more than made up for in cunning – hardly surprising as he'd been named Sutton Coldfield's Scoundrel in Residence the previous month. He sent Errol a good luck message for the Friday final – but when the young Solihull cyclist turned up he discovered that the race had been held the previous day, and in his absence the cunning Jeremy Fingest had been declared the winner.

Errol left college in 1997 and continued racing, and a succession of victories soon brought him to the attention of the British Track Cycling Federation. It appeared as though he might be an outside prospect for the 2000 Olympics team until a dreadful accident ruined his chances.

Out on a training bike-ride one morning Errol spotted an old woman laden with shopping trying to cross a busy road. Being of a generous nature he pulled over and offered to help carry her bags. Tragically for Errol, and Britain's Olympic cycling hopes, the old lady did not take kindly to his generous intervention. She refused to hand over her shopping to the muscular youth and instead began screaming at him, hitting him first with a stick and then with a tin of cat food to the side of the head. Reeling from the blows, Errol went tottering into the road, and the path of an articulated lorry. He spent the next eight months in traction in Solihull General Hospital, his Olympic dreams – like his bones and his bike – completely shattered.

Four years later Errol was back on a new bike and cycling well enough to make the squad for the 2004 Games, where he was selected for the 1,500 metres Magnum sprint. He arrived in Athens in fantastic shape, but once again Errol's generous spirit cost him dear. Just before his semi-final he was approached by an Italian cyclist, Stefano Macarinelli, who claimed he'd left his own bicycle back at home, and asked if he could borrow Errol's for a few minutes. He swore on his mother's grave that he'd give Errol the bike back straight after the race. That was the last Errol Pearce saw of Stefano Macarinelli or his bicycle, and it was only later he learned that the Italian cyclist's mother had been cremated, not buried. Errol Pearce had missed his great opportunity and, deprived of his bike, the gold medal went to an unknown Dane.

At the close of the Athens Olympics an angry Cycling Federation cut off Errol Pearce's lottery funding, and with no proper job to fall back on he soon drifted into destitution. Within a matter of months the Solihull Slingshot was living rough on the streets of London – the very ones made famous by Ralph McTell – when he was spotted by a documentary film-maker who was making a programme about cyclists living as tramps. It was typical of Errol Pearce that he should hand over the £10.83 he'd collected in his polystyrene cup that morning when the film-maker said he needed to buy a new lens cap. Not surprisingly Errol never saw the film-maker, or the lens cap, or the £10.83 ever again.

In February 2007 Errol Pearce formally announced his retirement from the sport in the tramps' section of *Cyclist's News*, just below an advert offering a stained sleeping bag for sale. A collection was organized for the former Olympic cyclist and raised over £300, although for some reason none of it ever reached Errol.

It was in the December of that year that Errol Pearce's luck finally changed for the better. He was keeping warm in a cyber-café when he received an email from a Nigerian person desperate to get rid of a fifty million pounds fortune, which for some reason was giving him a problem. Ever keen to offer his help, Errol answered the email, which surprisingly turned out to be genuine, and within a week he was fifty million pounds richer. Wealthy enough now to buy all the bikes he wants, it remains to be seen whether Errol Pearce can hang on to his newly found prosperity, or will get swindled out of it by an unscrupulous time-share salesman.

SIR HENRY ARDWELL-SMALL

Deck Quoits

Sir Henry Ardwell-Small – plain Henry until his father died – was born in Chittapur in India in 1889. His father, Sir Robert, was head of the Andhra Pradesh Civil Service, and while he did his best to keep the state from being buried under a mountain of red tape, it was difficult, as his chief task was the procurement of red-coloured tape. Henry's mother, Lady Roberta, did nothing whatsoever, as was the custom amongst the colonial wives. Instead she stayed indoors, terrified of tigers and of burning her lily-white skin, and pined for her beloved Norfolk.

To stimulate his wife, Sir Robert invested in a collection of beehives and several swarms of bees. Beekeeping was considered an acceptable hobby for the wives of colonial administrators in late Victorian India. The bee was not a culturally sensitive insect, while the protective clothing meant that a pale-skinned woman could venture out into the sunshine without worrying about her delicate complexion. Lady Roberta proved to be an accomplished beekeeper, and the colony of Indian Soft Bellied Bees – similar to the everyday bumblebee only with more velvety fur on its belly – produced gallons of exquisite honey.

All was bliss until 1905 when an unfortunate accident happened. Lady Roberta was set upon and mauled to death by a cunning tiger which had hidden itself behind a beehive. Sad though the young Henry was, his tears soon dried when he heard he'd inherited his mother's substantial swarm.

A few years later Henry Ardwell-Small's honey was the toast – and indeed *on* the toast – of India. In 1911, when King George V was crowned Emperor of India at the Delhi Durbar, Henry personally served the King-Emperor and Queen with very, very thin slices of bread and butter, topped with his finest honey. He even gave them a jar to take back to Buckingham Palace.

In 1913, Henry became Sir Henry on the death of his father. A wooden shelf, overburdened with box files of invoices and rolls of red tape, came crashing down on to Sir Robert's head. He'd hardly got used to his new title, when another honour came his way. Sir Henry Ardwell-Small was offered the post of Beekeeper Eminent by the Maharajah of Pallavas, a man renowned as the most cowardly prince in India. Such was the Maharajah's fear of tigers that he'd abandoned his palace and set up court on a luxury yacht, moored off the coast. Unperturbed, Sir Henry moved his hives on to the deck of the yacht, and began the job of creating the world's first nautical honey. The bees proved reluctant at first. Not only was the yacht moored several miles from the mainland, but the choppy waters of the Indian Ocean meant the hives would on occasion slither up and down the deck and distress the insects inside. But both parties persevered and the result was more wonderful honey, with slight undertones of salt.

With the bees largely self managing, Sir Henry was left

with plenty of time on his aristocratic hands. He had a long-held aversion to reading, so to while away the hours he began playing deck quoits – flinging rope-made rings for hours on end over wooden pegs. After seven years of sitting on deck Sir Henry was proficient enough at the game that he could toss quoits over pegs even during a howling monsoon without missing a single one.

This blissful existence came to an abrupt end in the summer of 1920 when Sir Henry was caught below deck in a compromising situation with the Maharajah's wife and a honey-dripper and was escorted from the yacht.

With the First World War over it was safe to go back to Britain, so Sir Henry bade farewell to India and, leaving his bees behind, set sail for England. He took up residence at the ancient family seat, Ardwell-Small Hall, near the town of Thetford in Norfolk. Here he lived an idyllic life, making honey, shooting things, tending his not inconsiderable estates and flinging the occasional quoit in the South Norfolk Pub Quoits League. Almost single-handedly he led the White Bull to two successive championships.

It is not known whether King George V was a follower of the South Norfolk Pub Quoits League, but he and Queen Mary were certainly both lovers of honey, and upon hearing that Sir Henry had settled only a few miles away from Sandringham appointed him the Royal Beekeeper. When the first batch of honey arrived, Queen Mary promptly dressed up as a milkmaid – one of her favourite pastimes – and sold it at the Sandringham Country Fair for sixpence a jar.

In the summer of 1923, midway through a match against the Swan and Spaniel, Sir Henry was summoned to London on a matter of some urgency. The nation was engaged in an unseemly trade war with France, the new Prime Minister Mr Baldwin told him. British jam and pork chops were rotting untouched in French ports, while French cheeses and champagne were maturing in a very large crate at Dover. Something needed to be done to break the deadlock. Sir Henry, a persuasive speaker, was despatched to Paris with several cases of his best honey to help alleviate the crisis.

The French promptly fell in love with Sir Henry Ardwell-Small's honey, and in return he found Paris very much to his liking. So favourable did he find it, in fact, that when the trade crisis was over, he decided to stay on, renting a comfortable townhouse near Montmartre. Here Sir Henry spent his time playing deck quoits and hosting lavish parties. He became very close friends with Josephine Baker, the celebrated American entertainer, who invented three new dances in honour of Britain's Royal Beekeeper. The 'Hive Jive', the very suggestive 'Pollen Pouch' and the still popular 'Black Bottom' all wowed the Parisian public, while her sultry paean to Sir Henry, 'My Honey Lover', scandalized British beekeeping.

Such had been Sir Henry's success in ending the trade war, however, that his peccadilloes were overlooked, most especially by the French. Indeed, the French President, M. Doumergue, suggested that Sir Henry might be honoured, perhaps with some sort of title. Sir Percy Grey, the British Ambassador, had a much better idea. Paris would be hosting the forthcoming Olympic Games. Why not add deck quoits to the programme? Nothing would more please the British government or Sir Henry Ardwell-Small. The event was duly added.

As expected, Sir Henry lobbed and tossed his way to an effortless gold medal. His Parisian circle of friends, including

Josephine Baker, Pablo Picasso and James Joyce, sat on the sidelines and cheered him to the rafters. Josephine Baker burst into song, while Picasso was so excited he stripped to his underpants, gave Sir Henry a piggy-back ride round the stadium and then painted a curious-looking portrait of him.

The all-conquering hero returned home to Norfolk and was greeted with a crisis. During his prolonged absence the royal family had run out of honey, and deprived of something to put on her toast – or an excuse to dress up as a milkmaid – the Queen had become irritable. The King, in turn, had passed on his own displeasure to 10 Downing Street, and before long Sir Henry Ardwell-Small's dereliction of duty – rather than his diplomatic or his sporting skills – were the subject of a heated debate in the House of Commons. He was censured by Parliament and pressured to resign as the Royal Beekeeper.

In truth though, there were no bees to keep. A particularly rampant strain of bee fungus had wiped out his entire swarm in 1925, and falling income from his estate meant he was hard-pressed to replace them. In 1926 he tried to import some Indian Soft Bellied Bees, but they proved ill-suited to the harsh Norfolk winter and perished.

The listless Sir Henry – now barred from the South Norfolk Pub Quoits League – sent a telegram to Josephine Baker, asking her to come to Thetford and marry him. If she received the message, she never replied.

Deck quoits was not retained for the Amsterdam Games of 1928, but even if it had been it is most unlikely that Sir Henry Ardwell-Small, with his chronic drink problem and convulsions, would have been able to retain his title.

He turned instead to growing cucumbers – enormous ones as it happens – but the royal family, and Queen Mary in particular, did not approve of rude-looking vegetables, and his monstrous efforts went largely unappreciated.

Sir Henry Ardwell-Small died, at the relatively tender age of forty-three, in 1932, when he stumbled and fell into a cold frame, severing an artery. He bled to death where he lay, undiscovered for a week, a bumper crop of mushrooms having sprung up in the blood-soaked manure.

Sir Henry was buried without fuss in the local church. There were less than half a dozen mourners present at the graveside – Josephine Baker and Pablo Picasso were not among them.

PAUL J. DRUMMOND

Sailing

It's often overlooked, but worth repeating, that Paul J. Drummond, the author of *101 Marvellous Things to do with Cormorants' Eggs* and *101 More Marvellous Things to do with Cormorants' Eggs* and twice voted Mr Gay Huddersfield, is also an exceptionally gifted yachtsman.

Apart from a few details Paul's upbringing was largely conventional. His mother worked as a nurse while his father ran the family ironmongery store. Nursing and hardware had been in the Drummond blood for generations, and Mr Drummond hoped that his son would one day inherit the business. An emotionally complex man, even by the standards of ironmongery, Mr Drummond expressed this desire mainly through Japanese kabuki, a passion which left his family and neighbours largely nonplussed. He continued, nevertheless, giving a particularly elaborate performance in 1997 by way of a double celebration. His son, Paul, had just turned sixteen – the legal age at which one can inherit an ironmongery shop in England – while Mr Drummond for his part had just finished constructing a yacht. He'd followed a 'Build Your Own Yacht' correspondence course, which had cost him the last few years of his life, not to mention a small fortune in weekly magazines.

The boat, a magnificent Sailfin class yacht, took up most of the back yard behind the little shop. Paul had been smitten as he'd watched his father building the yacht, a passion that ran alongside his burgeoning sexuality. He was desperate to sail in the boat, something that only proved possible when the ironmongery shop was demolished and the yacht dragged through the rubble and on to the main road. Pleased though he might be to see the boat finally freed, the destruction of his shop caused heartache for Mr Drummond, who exorcised his pain through a three-act kabuki performance. He performed it in the pouring rain, on the ruins of what was left of his shop.

Paul did not find the Sailfin an easy boat to master. His father had cancelled the correspondence course before the sailing instructions had arrived, and it took several dunkings in Coniston Water before the young man felt bold enough to take the boat on to the open sea. A few years later and the newly crowned Mr Gay Huddersfield was ready to race.

Paul J. Drummond's first competition was the Cowes Sailfin Classic in 2003. He trailed in some way down the field, but did manage to finish ahead of Pedro Martinez, the current world champion and a one-time Mr Gay Peru.

The Sailfin class was not included in the programme for the Athens Olympics the following year, but by the time Beijing arrived, in 2008, Paul J. Drummond was Britain's leading exponent. He was probably best known to the public, however, for his light-hearted book about cormorants, published earlier in the year, and his contribution to a saucy gay yachting calendar. He was Mr September.

A modest income from his book and calendar modelling,

plus a generous donation from the Cormorant Club of Great Britain (Gay Division), meant that Paul could devote his daytime hours to his sailing. In his night-time hours he preferred to do very different things altogether.

The overwhelming favourites for the Sailfin event, held at the Qingdao International Marina, were the German Heinrich Neff, the 2005 Mr Gay Frankfurt, and the 2002 Mr Wet T-Shirt of Helsinki, Pentti Koivulu. Paul J. Drummond was not ranked too far behind, but attracted little attention in the press. Even the yachting correspondent from *Gay Times* chose to ignore him.

The British sailing team had won two gold medals in Athens and were confidently expecting a similar haul in Beijing. Media focus was centred on Ben Ainslie, Iain Percy and the blonde girls. So when Paul's boat capsized on the first race, and he had to be pulled out of the water – as it happens by New Zealand's Ken Sloper, the ex-Mr Pride of Auckland – it looked as though the press had made the right decision.

Yet quietly and efficiently over the next eight races, Paul J. Drummond splished and splashed and gibed and tacked his way through the field. No yachtsman had managed to dominate the event and with one race remaining the destination of the medals was still unresolved. Neff the German, the Finn Koivulu, Paul J. Drummond and the experienced Canadian Cameron Flupe, who had a wife, were all in with a chance of winning the gold. The first man home would be crowned Olympic champion. By the third mark the German sailor had dropped off the pace, and as they rounded the halfway point the Canadian Flupe found himself becalmed in a grove of seaweed. In the end it came down to a straight race to the finish line between

Drummond and Koivulu, with the British yachtsman beating his Finnish rival by the thickness of a wet T-shirt.

Back in Huddersfield Paul's father was so delighted when he heard the news he slapped on some whiteface and gave an impromptu alfresco kabuki performance for the residents of Cooper Street.

Paul, for his part, celebrated long and hard that evening, finally going home with a bottle of Chinese sparkling wine and the phone number of a Slovenian yachtsman, drinking the former and mislaying the latter.

Since Beijing Paul J. Drummond has largely stayed out of the limelight. His appearances have been limited to a photo shoot (Mr October, 2010) and an article in *Seabird News*, where he was pictured catapulting a cormorant's egg off Tower Bridge (Number sixty-four in his first book).

It is to be hoped that Paul J. Drummond will defend his gold medal off Weymouth in 2012, but as the competition clashes with the Brisbane Mardi Gras his participation could well be in doubt.

CHUPO

Official Olympic Mascot

5 July 2005 was a day the country will never forget. Millions cheered and danced in the streets as the efforts of Seb Coe, Ken Livingstone and the saintly David Beckham brought the Olympic Games back to its spiritual home, the East End of London.

But as the nation rejoiced at the images of heartbroken Parisians, few spared a thought for those other British cities that had blazed the trail for London, bidding for the games and falling short. Both Birmingham and Manchester had previously thrown their municipal hats into the ring, and though now only a distant memory, so too had Bexhill-on-Sea.

It was on 12 April 1983 that the forward-thinking leader of Bexhill council, James Warren-Jones, first launched his ambitious – some might argue foolhardy – motion that the town should bid to host the 1992 Olympic Games. It was third on the agenda for that evening, sandwiched in between a debate on dog fouling and the quality of hot meals in the local hospital. The item was carried by fifty-nine votes to one – the lone dissenting voice being that of

Councillor Mark Blyth, Bexhill's maverick independent. Councillor Blyth's objections that the town was too small to host a festival of twenty-six sports featuring 10,000 athletes and play host to some half a million foreign tourists were dismissed as the ramblings of a killjoy. There were plenty of good provisions in the Bexhill area, Councillor Warren-Jones insisted – a swimming pool, a couple of football pitches, and the newly opened Warren-Jones Sports Centre complete with ice rink and climbing wall. Any facilities that didn't exist could doubtless be built by Warren-Jones and Sons (Builders) or any other firm of local contractors that won the tender. On the subject of how he proposed to accommodate the 500,000 visitors the Games might expect Councillor Warren-Jones was more sketchy, but did suggest there were plenty of decent hotels in the area, not to mention bed and breakfasts – all now fitted with the statutory fire escapes and smoke alarms. The Seaview, in Mount Street, he particularly recommended.

It wasn't a done deal, he told his fellow councillors, and there were no guarantees Bexhill-on-Sea would win. Other cities were also in the running to host the 1992 games – Buenos Aires, Tokyo, San Francisco and Barcelona to name but four. Yet what did they have to offer compared to the jewel of the Sussex coast?

The Bexhill bid ran into problems almost immediately, its first setback coming from nearby Hastings. The town, still reeling from its failure to secure the 1990 Commonwealth Games, voted unanimously at a council meeting to boycott the Olympics should they end up in Bexhill. They would offer neither facilities nor assistance. The second misfortune happened some two months later, and ended up becoming much more serious than the snub from Hastings. On fourteenth June, Councillor Warren-Jones unveiled his plan for Bexhill's Olympic Mascot. In his view there could be no better choice than Chucky the Chimp, the most popular attraction at Bexhill's 'Monkey Land'. He presented his fellow councillors with an image of Chucky dressed in a bright yellow waistcoat and carrying a pennant which featured a picture of the De La Warr Pavilion, the town's outstanding art-deco landmark. A million stuffed Chuckys could be mass produced, he enthused. It would not only bring some much needed employment to the area but would ensure that the name of Bexhill-on-Sea was even better known in the outside world than in was already.

Unfortunately for Councillor Warren-Jones, a faction in the council strongly objected to the choice of Chucky the Chimp. Councillor T.J. O'Grady thought the choice inappropriate, not least because 'Monkey Land' was owned by Councillor Warren-Jones. He'd also done his sums. According to Councillor O'Grady's calculations, when all the merchandising and spin-offs were taken into consideration Councillor Warren-Jones stood to benefit personally to the tune of some seventy-five million pounds – close to seventy-eight million pounds in today's money. It was nothing less than nepotism, said Councillor T.J. O'Grady, a sentiment also expressed by Councillors R.J. and J.P. O'Grady. They suggested an alternative mascot for the games in the shape of Popo the porpoise – a summer visitor which had been sighted off Bexhill's shingle beach and on one occasion caught by an unsuspecting fisherman. A show of hands was subsequently taken and the council found itself split down the middle, utterly deadlocked at thirty votes each. So, in the finest British tradition, a compromise was reached, and it was agreed that the town's two potential mascots might be combined as one. Thus was born the ghastly hybrid known as Chupo, with his chimpanzee's upper body and porpoise's rear end.

Councillor Warren-Jones gave the go-ahead for the mass production of mascots, and within a few weeks the first of several thousand fluffy Chupos rolled off the assembly line at the Frolic Factory, the headquarters of Warren-Jones Toys and Games.

A lavish festival was arranged – at ratepayers' expense – to celebrate Chupo's arrival and officially launch Bexhill's Olympic bid good and proper. Councillor Warren-Jones's wife, Mrs Warren-Jones, made an enormous sticky toffee pudding, the official dessert of Sussex. It may well have been Britain's largest ever – there were no previous records. Several pubs stayed open till midnight, while the Thompson Twins, a popular band at the time, performed several of their hits at the Sports Centre. But they were only the hors d'oeuvres for the real event. No sooner had the Twins finished playing than 3,000 locals who'd been waiting out of earshot rushed into the Sports Centre to see the half chimp-half porpoise being driven around the running track on the back of a flat-bed truck. Unfortunately, what should have been a triumph turned to tragedy when several children were crushed in the stampede to gather sweets flung by Chupo into the crowd. No one was seriously hurt, but the incident left a bitter taste – even allowing for all the sweets.

The identity of the individual inside the Chupo costume always remained a closely guarded secret. It was rumoured to be a junior member of the Warren-Jones family, although it was never proven – and perhaps that's just as well. An attempt to pull the chimp's head off, to see who was underneath, resulted in a full-blown brawl on stage at the BBC's *Sports Personality of the Year* show. Only the actions of a quick-witted producer, who played a collection of old clips and gaffes from yesteryear, prevented 15 million viewers seeing this unedifying spectacle. Chupo was cuffed around the ears – possibly by Barry McGuigan – bundled into a taxi and packed off back to Bexhill.

Chupo's next official appearance came at the opening ceremony for the 1984 Games, held in Los Angeles. Amidst much laughter and applause, mascots from the other four candidate cities – 'Gauchio' from Buenos Aires, 'Machiko' from Tokyo, San Francisco's 'Mr Smiles' and 'Cobi' representing Barcelona all marched and skipped their way around the stadium. Chupo, unable to stand on account of his fins, was dragged on a makeshift sledge by a couple of Bexhill scouts to a chorus of jeers and whistles. Before they'd even entered the stadium, the banner the chimp-cum-porpoise was supposed to have been carrying (bearing the legend: 'Bexhill – If Not Here, Where?') had been trodden on and torn in half by the clumsier of the two scouts. It took the hapless trio over an hour to complete the circuit, delaying the lighting of the flame and thus the start of the Games themselves by some forty-five minutes.

Only the happy coincidence of an unexplained power cut which deprived the town of TV pictures spared the good people of Bexhill-on-Sea this ignominy. By the time the electricity supply was restored, Chupo had been sent packing, and the one-eyed hoopla that was the Los Angeles Olympics had officially begun.

Chupo laid low for the remainder of 1984. An invitation to the next BBC's *Sports Personality of the Year* show, if sent, was declined.

The IOC's big decision, about where to host the 1992 Games, was made in Lausanne the following summer amidst great pomp and ceremony. The delegation from Bexhill-on-Sea, with Chupo kept at a discreet distance, held their breath – though in truth they did not have to do so for long. The town garnered only two votes in the opening round and were eliminated at the first hurdle.

At the next meeting of Bexhill Council – details of which have only recently emerged – Councillor Warren-Jones gave a valedictory speech concerning the town's Olympic bid. It was second on the agenda, and followed a debate on dog fouling. Despite Bexhill's defeat, the bidding process had not been a waste of time or money, he insisted. The seventy-eight million had been well spent, although as he personally hadn't stumped up the cash that was easy for him to say. Councillor Blyth, speaking against the motion, was unimpressed. Bexhill had indeed been put on the map – no one could deny that – but certainly not in a way that anyone would have wanted. Such was the force of Mr Blyth's arguments that a motion of no confidence in Councillor Warren-Jones was passed by fifty-eight votes to one. Talk of bidding for the 1996 Olympics were quietly dropped from the council's agenda. During the entire debate the name of Chupo, the unfortunate fusion of chimpanzee and porpoise, was not mentioned once.

The Bexhill Guy Fawkes bonfire that year was the biggest anyone could remember. It largely comprised an enormous mound of stuffed Chupo cuddly toys, surmounted with an effigy of Councillor James Warren-Jones. The flames from the bonfire could be seen in Hastings, and as luck would have it the wind blew the smoke in that direction too.

If it's any consolation, the IOC members, in their infinite

wisdom, awarded the Games of the XXV Olympiad to the city of Barcelona. The Games were one of the most successful ever held, and were not noticeably affected by the host city's choice of 'Cobi', a grotesque dog thing with a vaguely human shape, as their official mascot.

Over a million-and-a-half visitors came to the games; the members of Bexhill-on-Sea Council were not amongst them.

LADY CASSANDRA MOON

Billiards

Women's billiards gets a hard press these days. Most people could probably name no more than five or six top women players at very best. Seven at a push. Even if pressed it's most likely they wouldn't recall the greatest of them all: the player once dubbed the Femme Fatale of the Cradle Cannon and the Belle of the Baize, Lady Cassandra Moon.

Lady Cassandra Moon was born in 1882 in a moderately fashionable part of north London. Her father, Sir Austin Moon, the Liberal MP for Tufnell Park, was a highly respected sanitary expert who served as Minister for Taps in Mr Gladstone's 'Government of all the Plumbers'. His enormous, bushy black beard was the talk of the capital, and was so luxuriant and weighty it had to be carried by urchins on a barrow.

Lady Constance, Cassandra's mother, took next to no interest in her husband's work or indeed in her family, preferring instead the company of writers and artists. Some famous names of the day made frequent visits to the Moon household, almost always when Sir Austin was away on business, which was most of the time.

An only child, Cassandra received no formal education. Instead she was tutored by a succession of anonymous governesses, who presumably taught her – in addition to deportment, sensibility and swooning – the finer points of billiards. By the turn of the century, and her eighteenth birthday, she was highly proficient at the game, and could be seen night after night at her father's billiard table racking up breaks in the tens of thousands. According to George Bernard Shaw, who popped in one evening when Sir Austin wasn't there, the only reason Lady Cassandra didn't damage her back with so much leaning over the table was because she was strapped into a whalebone corset. It not only helped her posture, but also contributed to her devastating cueing action.

At the general election in September 1900 the Conservatives were returned to office with a thumping great majority. So thumping great, in fact, that Sir Austin Moon lost his Tufnell Park seat, never again to return to Westminster. As a consequence he spent more time with his daughter, until one thrashing too many at the billiard table made him pack her off to Cambridge. Billiards was a popular sport at Cambridge in late Victorian England. It was believed that billiards concentrated the mind, and students were encouraged to spend as much time as possible playing the game. Cassandra was only too happy to heed this advice, and spent a blissful three years in various smoke-filled rooms and vice dens, playing billiards to her heart's content and picking up all manner of unfortunate habits, not the least of which was her failure to attend a single lecture.

With her peach-like complexion, wonderful potting technique and obscenely rich father, Lady Cassandra Moon was one of the most eligible women in Cambridge. She spurned all advances, however, preferring to spend her time bent over the billiard table. It wasn't wasted effort either. Between 1901 and 1903 she won the Maud Pascoe Shield – that most venerated of varsity billiard trophies – on three successive occasions.

But there was a regrettable footnote to the girl's victories. It was rumoured that there had been funny goings on in Cassandra's rooms, possibly involving the Honourable F.T. Smallman, the rummest cove in Cambridge. Then, in the 1903 Shield decider against the dowager Emily Simms-Dudley, some observers noted that Cassandra was glassy-eyed and deathly pale, shaking and sometimes incoherent – although fortunately it had no effect on her game. Cornered by a billiards journalist who asked her if she'd 'dabbled', Cassandra quoted her mother's friend, the controversial Irish playwright Oscar Wilde: 'Ducks dabble – I consume.'

In 1904 Sir Austin Moon died unexpectedly on a trip to inspect some sluice gates near Felixstowe. His long beard got caught in a bilge pump and he was dragged under the water. Cassandra was temporarily heartbroken and entered a period of lavish mourning, paid for by her extravagant inheritance. She began spending her money like it grew on trees, which it did in a way, as her father owned numerous apple orchards in Herefordshire.

She may have had a place in high society, but the world of competitive billiards was a cul-de-sac for Lady Cassandra Moon. There was no women's billiards championship to speak of, and indeed the only reference to her in the trade magazine *Billiards World* – apart from mentioning her vacant expression and penchant for aromatic hand-rolled Turkish cigarettes – was when she was made 'Sweetheart of the

Month' in the January 1907 issue. But that was soon to change.

Like many other ladies of breeding and refinement, Lady Cassandra had become attracted to the suffragette movement, with its talk of votes for the better class of woman, and she put herself about with great gusto. She knocked off several policemen's helmets, and in 1910 poked the Prime Minister, Mr Balfour, with her billiard cue. Then, in 1911 at Windsor Castle, Cassandra caused a to-do when she threw herself on the King's pigeon basket as a protest. Many regarded it as an empty gesture, which it was in some respects. There were no pigeons left in the basket. They'd all raced off – probably up north somewhere.

The ever resourceful Emmeline Pankhurst, the suffragette in chief, wondered if she might not be able to harness this enthusiasm. She therefore instigated the first women's professional billiards championship, Mrs Pankhurst's only proviso being that the trophy – made of best Welsh pewter – should be restricted to women who'd chained themselves to railings. When she heard the news Cassandra Moon headed straight for 10 Downing Street and clamped herself there. It was Cassandra's misfortune that her selfless act coincided with a deputation of Cockney angle-grinders on a visit to the Prime Minister, and she was cut free within a matter of minutes.

It came as no surprise when Lady Cassandra Moon won the Suffragette's Trophy. Her chief rivals – such as Sylvia Spry and Dame Alice Collier – simply weren't in her league. So with the title in the bag, and an army of posh women supporters behind her, Cassandra threw down a challenge to the world billiards champion himself, Melbourne Inman – no relation to the camp comedy actor John Inman, famous for his catchphrase, 'I'm free'. As it turned out Melbourne Inman wasn't free, and certainly not prepared to risk his great reputation against an opponent who wore corsets and a skirt.

In October 1912, Cassandra headed to Stockholm as the overwhelming favourite to win the Olympic gold medal in the inaugural women's billiards event. But it was not to be, and the British aristocrat ended up suffering the biggest shock, and possibly the only defeat, of her entire playing career. It was a tactical error entirely of her own making. No sooner had she entered the billiard hall to take on her first opponent, than Lady Cassandra took out a stout pair of handcuffs and clamped herself to the first man she could find. He turned out to be a visiting minor royal, Crown Prince Henrik of Denmark. Etiquette prevented either a pair of bolt cutters or a welding torch being used in case it damaged the royal wrist, so Cassandra had to play her match against the German, Fraulein Krinkelpumpf, with her left arm seriously inconvenienced. She was obliged to play a number of extremely difficult cannons in order that the Crown Prince was not yanked endlessly across the billiard table. Despite the handicap of the Crown Prince, Cassandra won the game and her next one too. But it took two days, and some delicate sleeping arrangements, before a diplomatic note came back from Denmark with the news that the King had given permission for the Swedes to use a cutting machine to free his son. But as far as Lady Cassandra's chances were concerned, the damage had been done. Although she won her remaining three matches, under the arcane rules of billiards (which in those days still used the Knibbs-Protheroe scoring system), the result was calculated by the total number of points scored, rather than matches won. During the two victories Lady Cassandra had achieved whilst chained to Crown Prince Henrik, she'd failed to score heavily enough, and in the final analysis that proved decisive. The gold medal went to a local girl, Lena Ulvskog, and Lady Cassandra Moon had to settle for a disappointing silver.

Despite her misfortune the Filly of the Felt-Topped Table found time to have a splendid country house, Half Butt, built near Marlow in Buckinghamshire, where she entertained long and lavishly. It was there, in 1915, during a billiards weekend, that she met Charles Peruzzi, the socialite and furniture designer, through their mutual friend Virginia Woolf. Peruzzi had created a radical new form of wood glue, and Cassandra, despite having only the vaguest interest in adhesives, found herself drawn to the young man. The relationship survived a number of scandals – mostly involving illicit substances – until the 1920 billiards championships. During the final Lady Cassandra's favourite and recently re-glued cue fell to pieces, and Peruzzi was shown the door.

The 1920s, and indeed the 1930s, were sad and desperate years for Lady Cassandra Moon. Women might have got the vote, but billiards, once so fashionable, had fallen into a decline from which it has never really recovered. What's more, she was none too judicious in her choice of friends, entertaining such ne'er-do-wells as Ezra Pound and Oswald Mosley, and talking racial superiority and billiards long into the night.

When war broke out she found herself interned – or in her case held under house arrest, as she was an aristocrat. She was mostly left alone, but following Dunkirk a jeering mob invaded Half Butt. Although Lady Cassandra herself was left unharmed, her billiard cues were carted off, snapped and burned in Marlow town square. After the nation had seen off the Nazis in 1945, the sixty-three-year-old Cassandra Moon was released into a world which no longer cared about her. The billiards authorities took it considerably further than that, and hired a little old man to scratch her name off all the trophies she'd won. It took him three days.

Lady Cassandra Moon spent her remaining years in long, slow decline, worn out by decades of substance abuse. She died in the sweltering summer of 1976, at ninety-five years of age. The vicar at her cremation was the Reverend Alan Symes, the top-ranked billiards-playing clergyman in the Church of England. He said a few nice words, but none of them were about Lady Cassandra. After the service the small clutch of mourners, including the Reverend Symes, had to be briefly sent to hospital. The coffin, it transpired, had been jam-packed with exotic smoking material. It was a final two-fingered gesture from beyond the urn.

THE GREAT GOLANDO

800 Metres; Shot Put; Free Pistol; Weightlifting (Middleweight); Boxing (Middleweight); Parallel Bars (Gymnastics); Sprint Cycling; Rowing (Single Sculls); Canoeing (Kayak Singles)

Open almost any magazine in the 1920s and you'd have seen an image of the Great Golando. His serious countenance – fingers pressed to powerful temples – peered out from countless pages. The familiar picture accompanied an advert for a course of self improvement that the Great Golando called Dynamic Mentalism. It was, he claimed, the ability to influence events using nothing more than the power of the mind. For a small consideration, which purchased the booklet, wrist supports, dumb-bells and singlet, the secrets of the universe could be yours. At only 3/6d it seemed almost too good to be true. By 1927, thanks to all those 3/6d postal orders, the Great Golando was a millionaire. The following year he was in Amsterdam, standing on the start line for the men's 800 metres, in his own mind at least, the overwhelming favourite for the gold medal.

To anyone who knew the Great Golando in his youth,

when he was plain Timothy Munnings, such athletic prowess would no doubt have come as a shock. As a pudgy schoolboy at Gravelgates Secondary, in St Albans, the best young Munnings could ever achieve was second from last in the sack race. He only managed that because Williamson's club foot got tangled in the cloth, and he tripped and smashed his bottle glasses. From no-hope athlete to potential Olympic champion in just a few years was quite some transformation.

The first adverts promoting the merits of Dynamic Mentalism appeared in the pages of *Conquest* magazine in October 1925, when Munnings would have been about 20 years old. Before long they were regular features in such disparate publications as *Sea Dog*, *Practical Housewife*, *The Magnet*, *Busy Beaver* and *Women's Things*. The St Albans sorting office soon became clogged with sacks full of 3/6d postal orders and requests, while a steady stream of devotees made the pilgrimage to the town, camping outside the Great Golando's ordinary suburban house, hoping to catch a glimpse of the man himself. Occasionally a pretty woman would be summoned inside, usually late in the evening. A second batch of adverts soon followed the first, each offering testimonies extolling the virtues of Dynamic Mentalism. The country, it seemed, couldn't get enough of it.

But one man who wasn't satisfied was a Tory MP, Sir Claude D'Aubigny Stretton. He'd spent his parliamentary career trying to expose quacks and frauds, and suspected that there was more to Dynamic Mentalism than met the eye. Or more pertinently, a lot less. He believed it to be nothing more than a money-making scheme, a belief which was confirmed when his package arrived from St Albans.

While the dumb-bells, wrist support and singlet were inside, there was no booklet about the inner workings of Dynamic Mentalism; no clue as to how to unlock the untapped potential of the brain. There was merely a note saying 'Secrets of the universe to follow'.

It was too much for Sir Claude. Using his power of parliamentary privilege he denounced Munnings as a fraud and issued a series of challenges, all of which were either ignored or dismissed in high-handed fashion. A request that the Great Golando manifest his powers in front of a House of Commons select committee was similarly pooh-poohed. There was no need, scoffed the master of Dynamic Mentalism – certainly not when Sir Claude D'Aubigny Stretton's own daughter Clarinda had already experienced those powers at first hand. Sir Claude was furious at this breach of etiquette. He'd gone to great lengths to prevent his estranged daughter's waywardness becoming public knowledge, and vowed his revenge. His first step was the introduction of a Green Paper aimed at curbing the excesses of cheats and bounders. His second step would spell the beginning of the end for the Great Golando.

In early 1928 the cream of British sport was preparing for the forthcoming Olympics in Amsterdam. Interrupting a debate on the gassing of badgers, Sir Claude D'Aubigny Stretton made a stirring speech calling on the greatest British minds to work together in the service of the nation. There was clearly no greater mind in Britain than that of the Great Golando, declared Sir Claude, and he recommended that the master of Dynamic Mentalism be sent to the Netherlands to represent the United Kingdom in the Olympic Games. Johnny Foreigner would surely be no match for a chap with his self-professed talents – why there was no telling how much gold and glory he might win, what with all the sustained powers of the universe at his beck and call. There was a tumultuous cheering in the House, the badgers were quickly forgotten and a shell-shocked Munnings was hastily despatched to Amsterdam.

The Great Golando arrived to learn that an ambitious programme had been set for him. After presumed victory in the 800 metres he was scheduled for the shot put that same afternoon, where he would also win gold. The free pistol would follow the next day, with the weightlifting (middle-weight class) in the evening. The opening rounds of the boxing tournament (middleweight division) began on the Wednesday, after which he could transport himself over to the Gymnastics Hall and win the parallel bars event. On Thursday morning he was pencilled for the sprint cycling, with rowing (single sculls) in the afternoon. He would be given a day off on Friday, before finishing off with a gold medal in the canoeing (kayak singles) on the Saturday. If he wished to compete in any more events, he was of course free to do so.

There was understandably an enormous interest in his first event, the 800 metres. Everyone was curious to see how the squat chubby Briton, with his raised collar and monogrammed shirt, would fare. Would Dynamic Mentalism make a mockery of Olympic competition? Would the Great Golando completely rewrite the record books? As soon as the starter fired the gun, the answer became abundantly clear. While the other athletes began running round the cinder track, the Great Golando remained on the start line, his fingers tightly pressed to his temples. He was still there, rooted to the spot, when the race finished nearly two minutes later. The cheers for

Douglas Lowe, the British winner, were almost drowned out by jeers and catcalls aimed at the silly-looking man in the silk shorts and cape.

Within the hour the Great Golando's name had been withdrawn from the entry list for shot put, free pistol, weightlifting (middleweight class), boxing (middleweight division), parallel bars, rowing (single sculls) and canoeing (kayak singles). The next day someone remembered he was down for the sprint cycling and took his name off that, too. Two days later he was reported to be back in St Albans. How he returned home is not certain, although it might be assumed it was not through the wonderful powers of Dynamic Mentalism.

The magazine adverts stopped immediately, the lovelorn women left the front garden, and Dynamic Mentalism went from being the craze of 1928 to the least talked about thing of 1929. It's believed that Munnings lost most of his money in the stock market collapse of the early 1930s. Clearly no amount of pressing his fingertips to his temples enabled him to see what was about to happen.

After many years of being forgotten, the Great Golando re-emerged in 1971, seemingly a changed man. A lay preacher by this time, he tried to set up a course of keep-fit exercises with a biblical theme. Unfortunately, Pontius Pilates never caught on, and had vanished before the year was out.

There aren't too many sightings of the Great Golando after that. He was reported to be in Brighton in 1974, while in 1983 there was an unconfirmed sighting of him in the Trowbridge area. In all likelihood, though, the Great Golando was dead by then, unloved and unmourned. Of course, it's just about possible that he's still alive today. If he was, he'd be over a hundred years old, and living proof that he really had discovered the secret of Dynamic Mentalism after all.

ERIC SOWERBY AND PIGEONMILK BOB

Greyhound Racing

There are few sights in sport more captivating than a racing greyhound in full flight. To witness those sleek, streamlined beasts tearing around the track like hairy, heat-seeking missiles is quite something. Mick the Miller, Scurlogue Champ and Pie-Eyed Pete have all worn the jacket with distinction. Yet of all the greyhounds Great Britain has produced surely none has generated such pride as the Lightning Flash of Trimdon Colliery, Pigeonmilk Bob – the animal that raised the spirits of the nation in the austerity London Olympics of 1948.

Trimdon Colliery, in County Durham, doesn't exist anymore. Like most of the nation's coal mines, it's been grassed over and turned into a country park. A rare yellow-banded wryneck, a drab-looking songbird blown over from the Urals, was spotted there in 1999. For the first time in more than fifty years, it made the name of Trimdon Colliery national news.

Before it closed in 1946, Trimdon was an unusual pit, with thin narrow seams of coal that sloped gently downwards.

The terrain proved unsuitable for an underground railway, and too low for ponies. So instead, the miners tied little wheeled baskets to the backs of greyhounds, filled them with coal and sent them back up to the surface. Despite reasonable living quarters and plenty of food, it was no real life for a dog, and the wretched animals had a very poor record when it came to longevity. Of course, the Greyhound Protection League would have had a field day had they known about the practice, but in the early 1940s, under the shadow of war, animal rights wasn't much of an issue.

The man responsible for the pit greyhounds was Eric Sowerby, and when the mine gates clanged shut for the last time in 1946 he took the two remaining dogs home with him. The older of them, Durham Dan, unaccustomed to daylight, died almost immediately. But the other dog, the brindle-coloured Pigeonmilk Bob, seemed to thrive on the damp, smog-filled, north-east air. The Sowerby family loved Bob and treated him like a prince – a prince that ate dog biscuits at any rate. Bob also developed a voracious appetite for offcuts, and devoured as much liver, cow heel, tripe, brawn sausages and sheep's heads that Eric could put in front of him. Before long he was eating the Sowerbys – who were living on social security – out of humble house and home.

Eric Sowerby was intelligent enough to realize that if none of the human beings in the family could work, they did at least have an able-bodied dog who could earn his keep. So, in October 1946, Pigeonmilk Bob was entered in a grey-hound race in Consett, where he surprised his owner and the other five dogs by winning handsomely. The long hours toiling underground had giving him marvellously strong leg muscles, and he skipped around the cinder track like poetry in a yellow waistcoat. Eric had been brave enough to back his dog at odds of 20–1 with every penny he possessed, and went home with ten shillings in his pocket. The next day he treated his family, and they all ate liver, cow heel, tripe, brawn sausages and sheep's heads – not just Pigeonmilk Bob.

Bob won his next outing at Hartlepool dog track, and the one after that. Within six months he'd won no fewer than fourteen races, and the Sowerbys had become the best-known family in Consett. Unfortunately, with fame came jealousy, and in the cash strapped north-east of the 1940s, anyone with a successful greyhound was seen as uppity, and too big for their boots – an ill-considered criticism, as Eric Sowerby had rather small feet. Not that people looked at Eric's feet – they pointed instead at the bottle of champagne he'd bought for his wife June to celebrate their wedding anniversary. It was believed by many to be the first champagne ever purchased and drunk in County Durham, and the empty bottle later ended up on display in Consett Museum.

In the summer of 1947, while out for a training run on the windswept beach at Seaton Carew, Pigeonmilk Bob's keen eyes noticed a tragedy unfolding in the cold grey water. An inflatable lilo was being washed out to sea, and there were two children clinging on to it. With no thought for his own safety, the greyhound plunged into the icy North Sea and dog-paddled his way out to the flimsy rubber raft. Gripping it gently with the gummy part of his mouth so as not to cause a puncture, and summoning up all his doggy strength, he towed the infants back to the safety of the shore. Eric promptly clipped the children around the ear (which you could do in 1947) and told them to take better care next time.

Pigeonmilk Bob became a hero overnight, not just among the local folk, but throughout the country and beyond. In the USSR a set of stamps was issued honouring canine heroes of socialist labour. The five-rouble stamp featured Bob splashing in the water, while the ten-rouble depicted Pavluk, the Aral pug who'd found a family of subversives hiding in a hay barn.

In the wake of the rescue, Eric and Pigeonmilk Bob were invited to London, where the dog was entered in the Greyhound Derby. Everybody who was anybody in the greyhound world was there that night – Henry Gallagher was in the commentary box describing the action for the BBC, and members of the London underworld were out in force. The only notable absentee was Grandma Sowerby, who'd eaten some margarine that had gone off, and had one of her funny turns. Although he was comfortably the outsider, Bob showed the other greyhounds a clean pair of heels and came home to win the prestigious cup. Half an hour later he'd been stripped of the prize. A random test revealed the dog had tested positive for brine, and in those far-off – some might say ignorant – days salt water was a prohibited substance in greyhound racing. Eric Sowerby was bitterly upset and complained to the track authorities. 'Big Jim' Sweyne, who owned the dog who'd originally finished second, promised Eric he'd investigate it personally – although after Eric discovered this meant going for a long car journey with 'Big Jim' and his friends and having his legs broken, he let the matter drop.

Pigeonmilk Bob's superb running had not gone unnoticed, however, and drew him rave reviews in the leading greyhound magazine, *Flat Cap Gazette*. Bert Pickles, the controversial xylophonist and greyhound racing expert, reckoned the dog was a world beater, and began drumming up a campaign to have the sport included in the upcoming Olympic Games, to be held in London. Pickles argued that it would let northerners feel they had some sort of stake in the Olympics, even if that wasn't really true. Besides, Wembley Stadium had the mother of all greyhound tracks, and with 100,000 spectators to cheer them on, the dogs would go at it hammer and tongs. The authorities seemed convinced – especially when informed that Pigeonmilk Bob would be a likely gold medal winner – and less than two months before the start of the Games they announced the inclusion of a greyhound race.

But Eric Sowerby was not so convinced. He'd fallen in with Herbie Parker, a leading animal agent and man about town, who persuaded the Consett man that Pigeonmilk Bob was a goldmine on legs, and that he could earn a fortune on the lucrative American dog-racing circuit. Parker also told Eric he had the makings of a teen-idol crooner – like Frank Sinatra – even though the ex-pitman was fifty-three, balding and no oil painting. Determined to head to the States, it was only a vigorous letter-writing campaign in *Flat Cap Gazette* that persuaded Eric Sowerby to postpone his dream of crooning super-stardom until after the Olympics.

The Games saw the greatest festival of dog racing that the civilized world had ever seen. Greyhounds came from all around the globe: from North and South America, Australia, Europe and the other continents too. The only major nation missing was Germany – the Second World War's losers – which deprived Fritzel Schnitzel, the Teutonic Windhund, of a triumph on British soil. Six dogs qualified for the grand final, but there were two clear favourites:

Slinky Pinky, an American dog that lived up to its name, and Pigeonmilk Bob.

As the animals were led around the arena and into their traps, the audience fell quiet – then as the mechanical hare set off, and the gate went up, 100,000 voices roared as one. The Australian dog, Captain Bacon, took a narrow lead by the first corner, and at the end of the lap was still holding it. But as the antipdeoan animal tired, Slinky Pinky took over in front. The Irish dog, Galloping Galway, followed with Pigeonmilk Bob in hot pursuit. The Wembley crowd, hopeful of a patriotic home victory, cheered nervously as the dogs rounded the final corner, with Pigeonmilk Bob still in the bronze medal position. But the gallant, life-saving, former pit greyhound never knew when he was beaten and, as he strained every last sinew in his aerodynamic body, he managed to pass both Galloping Galway and Slinky Pinky to flash across the finish line in first place. Wembley Stadium erupted.

Eric Sowerby and Pigeonmilk Bob returned to County Durham to a rapturous welcome. All jealousies and petty hatreds were forgotten as the people of Consett applauded their Olympic heroes. But along with his gold medal, Eric had something far more sinister in his pocket – it was a letter from the recently constituted National Coal Board. The NCB insisted that the nation's favourite greyhound belonged to them and that Sowerby had taken him without their permission. When he refused to return the dog – or the gold medal – the Coal Board slapped an injunction on him, preventing the dog from taking part in any further races, making any personal appearances or leaving the country.

NCB v Sowerby opened at the High Court in the summer of 1949. To begin with, there was huge public interest in the case, but as the dispute dragged on and on, curiosity inevitably waned. The only moment that caught the headlines came in August, when Pigeonmilk Bob was summoned to the witness box. Cross-questioned on the basis of two barks for yes and one bark for no, the day's proceedings ended in chaos when the animal refused to stop barking.

After some five and a bit years of legal to-ing and fro-ing – a world record for a case involving disputed greyhound ownership – the jury finally found in Eric Sowerby's favour, and granted him custody of Pigeonmilk Bob. Sadly, it made little difference to the dog, which had passed away in 1953. But rather than consign him to a burial, Eric Sowerby contacted taxidermist Henry Bryce-Hamilton, the so-called 'Stuffer to the Stars', who had the dog crammed full of sawdust. The Fleet-Footed Fido spent the last twelve months of the case on an attractive elm plinth, his glass eyes fixed on the public gallery.

Pigeonmilk Bob did end up on the other side of the Atlantic after all – taken by Eric and his family to tour on the lucrative stuffed-dog circuit. They did rather well, and made enough money to retire in some comfort in 1969. Eric Sowerby's only regret was that his beloved greyhound wasn't there to see it.

WELLESLEY FAGGE

Cricket

Wellesley Fagge was one of British sport's last great Corinthians. Born in 1945, at Wyncoates Manor in Northamptonshire, he was devoted to his father whose guiding philosophy was a simple one: always play fair, and give your opponent a fighting chance. Wellesley experienced his father's credo, most devastatingly in 1956, during a safari holiday to Tanganyika. The Fagge were attacked by a rampaging bull elephant, yet despite having a gun, Mr Fagge steadfastly refused to shoot on the grounds that it was the off-season for rampaging bull elephants. As a result he and a further eleven members of his family were trampled or crushed to death. Only young Wellesley escaped the carnage, and when he'd fully recovered from his tusk injuries he was packed off back to England and Bishop Grindley's, one of the best public schools in Northamptonshire.

His father had been a major patron of cricket in the county, and no sooner had he settled into the school than Wellesley was made captain of the first team. It was a controversial decision. He was a twelve-year-old lad in a team full of eighteen-year-olds and, it's fair to say, somewhat out of his depth. In Bishop Grindley's first game, against Harrow, he was skittled first ball, and ended with the less than impressive bowling figures of 0 for 241. The headmaster urged Wellesley to take net practice with the rest of the team, but to young Fagge that was tantamount to cheating and he refused. His poor performance was explained in the school magazine as a combination of bad luck and youthful nerves. Unfortunately things didn't improve in his next match, against King Charles II School of Melton Mowbray, home of the pork pie. The school was known for its generous cricketing teas, which generally centred on the savoury pork treat. Wellesley, as selfless as ever, stood aside to allow the other boys to devour the pies, and by the time he'd consented to eat there was nothing left but crumbs. On the pitch, he fared even worse. In the second over, attempting what should have been an easy catch, he was hit square on the head by the ball and knocked out cold. When the heavens opened up a few minutes later and the game was abandoned, the unconscious Wellesley was left prostrate in the middle of the pitch.

Thanks to the munificence of the Fagge Bequest, Wellesley remained school cricket captain for the next six years, despite the fact that his performances didn't noticeably improve. When his education finished he moved to London, keen to experience what his father had referred to as 'the benefits of hard work' and fulfil a useful place in society. After turning down countless better jobs in favour of other candidates he finally found employment as a tar tapper for Wellingborough Council. This involved tramping the streets with buckets of tar, finding holes in the road, filling them with the sticky black goo and then walloping them with a shovel to the satisfaction of absolutely nobody.

In addition to his back-breaking labouring work, Wellesley also kept his hand in at cricket. His father's good name meant that doors opened at Northamptonshire County Cricket Club, and even Wellesley's unimpressive playing statistics didn't hinder his chances. He joined the club in 1965, and within a year had been made captain. Noticing his rather unorthodox grip, which was more used to holding a tar bucket, Ted Farmer, the Northants coach, tried to teach Wellesley how to hold the bat and the ball. But Wellesley, ever true to his beliefs, blocked his ears and hummed, and didn't hear a word.

In his first game, against Kent, Wellesley was unlucky. Perhaps he was distracted by the sound of swans fighting on the river or maybe the liveliness of the wicket caught him off guard. Either way, he was out first ball, swishing hopelessly at a medium-paced yorker. He bowled just a single over, at a cost of some twenty-eight runs, before he tripped and broke an ankle. Wellesley's stubborn refusal to let the club doctor treat his injury had a detrimental effect on his cricket. He missed the remainder of the season and walked for the rest of his life with a pronounced limp.

As he hobbled about Northamptonshire recuperating, Wellesley began to enjoy some sporting success – perhaps the first in his life. Under archaic medieval law the county still permitted cock fighting, and Wellesley not only found himself elected president of the society, but also acquired an exceptionally aggressive cockerel. Feathery Frank went undefeated throughout the entire 1967 cock-fighting season, and decisively out-pecked Lord Wansdyke's gallant bird to win the Daldry Cock-Fighting Cup.

Wellesley Fagge didn't take to the cricket pitch again until 1969, when Glamorgan were the visitors. Tragically, whilst walking to the crease he slipped on a rather dewy patch of grass and his ankle went again. Unable to play any more cricket Wellesley bravely carried on tar tapping, his shattered ankle resting on the kerb. But while his leg slowly mended, his back deteriorated, unable to withstand the constant thumping of the shovel on the road. He might have benefited from better equipment, but Wellesley would never permit himself to have first pick of the shovels, and he was usually left with a half-broken one and a rusty bucket.

Over the next ten years, Wellesley Fagge played very little cricket. A succession of debilitating injuries, which seemed to take forever to heal, prevented him from taking the field on more than two or three occasions. While a first-class wicket eluded him, he did manage to score a total of four runs in a game against Essex in 1973. Trying to protect himself from a moderately paced delivery, Wellesley's bat somehow struck the ball, which ran all the way to the boundary. The sparse crowd rose to their feet, sitting down again when he was out next ball. By 1979 Northamptonshire had almost forgotten about Wellesley Fagge – so much so that he'd been demoted to vice-captain of the club.

But while the Northants Corinthian was recuperating, and enjoying the benefits of modern technology in the shape of a plastic bucket, fate was playing a strange trick. It was announced in the sports pages of the Russian newspaper *Pravda* that cricket – a game once denounced by Stalin as an imperialist conspiracy – would be reintroduced for the 1980 Moscow Games. Cricket had been a banned sport in the Soviet Union since the time of Stalin. No one can be sure where the mass-murdering dictator's dislike for cricket originated, but the best evidence suggests it began in Kiev in 1943. Playing in a friendly match against a Winston

Churchill XI, he was controversially out leg before wicket off the bowling of Field Marshall Montgomery having scored a useful thirty-four runs. It was the second of Monty's double – a few overs previously he'd had Lavrenti Beria, the head of the Communist Party, caught at deep extra cover by Churchill himself. Stalin took his defeat at cricket very badly. It strained the relationship between the USSR and Britain during the darkest days of the Second World War, and almost certainly explains the pogrom against the town of Vladikavkutsk, in the heart of cricket-playing Russia. By 1979 though, all that had been forgotten, and the cricketing nations of the world all signed up to compete in Moscow. Professionals were ineligible in those days, of course, so that ruled out the likes of Botham, Gower and Willis competing – but it left the door wide open for the best of British amateurs.

When the Soviets invaded Afghanistan in late 1979, most of the world's cricketing nations decided to join the Americans in their boycott of the Moscow Games. Only the British held out, although by the time the Olympics arrived, there were almost no amateur cricketers who were willing to go. In desperation, a member of the selection committee phoned Wellesley Fagge. Wellesley, as usual, needed asking twice. It wasn't until he was convinced that everyone else had been approached, that there really wasn't anybody else, and that Wellingborough Council would give him the time off work, that he agreed to go – and go as captain.

The motley selection of cricketers that wore the British whites fared poorly. Wellesley's expensive bowling meant they lost to Czechoslovakia, a nation of cricketing novices whose opening batsman had to be shown how to hold his bat. It was only a narrow victory over Tanzania – in which

Wellesley sustained an injury and was unable to bat or bowl – that helped them progress to the next round. Amazingly, a week later, and still deprived of their skipper, the British team had reached the final of the competition. Now only the host nation stood between them and cricketing gold.

During those seven days, Wellesley's persistently injured ankle healed itself sufficiently for him to declare himself fit to play against the Soviets. His team mates tried to convince him to rest a while longer – preferably until after the final – but, for once, Wellesley Fagge wouldn't hear of it. Nothing would prevent him from playing. So, despite a number of mysterious near accidents, involving a hammer, a rabid dog and a chainsaw, it was Wellesley who led out the team to do battle for the cricket gold medal.

The British batted first, and lost quick wickets to some strange decisions. In one over, three batsmen were given out by the Bulgarian umpire, officiating in his first ever cricket match. With the score at a wretched forty-three for four, Wellesley Fagge hobbled out to bat.

Throughout his career, it must be said, Wellesley had hardly distinguished himself at cricket. In fifteen years he'd scored a total of four runs and never taken so much as a solitary wicket. Yet for once, and on the highest stage imaginable, he somehow found a talent that no one had suspected lay within him, and played the game of his life. Accompanied at the crease first by J.H.T. Charming and then by another Suffolk cricketer, R.F. Rapunzel, Wellesley Fagge played what can only be described as a fairy-tale innings. He stroked the ball magnificently, timing his shots to perfection, and giving the Bulgarian officials no excuse to give him out. By the end of the team's allotted forty overs they had scored a total of 212 runs, of which Wellesley had managed a magnificent ninety-eight not out.

However, it soon became obvious, as the Soviet team batted, that it was not going to be Britain's day. Decision after decision went against the team, and Wellesley had at least six perfectly good dismissals ruled out as no balls. The team gradually lost heart, and conceded the winning runs to the Russians with a couple of overs to spare. Such was the team's disappointment that they finally staged their own boycott – refusing to turn up for the medal ceremony and leaving the silver part of the podium empty.

Despite his moment of glory, Wellesley Fagge never played another game of first-class cricket. During his absence his registration papers had been consumed in an unexplained fire in the Northamptonshire offices, and the club was unwilling to offer him a new contract.

In 1984, Wellesley Fagge died, lost at sea. He was on his way to start a new life in Australia, where the weather was nicer and a huge road-building programme meant that the tar-tapping possibilities were almost endless. According to *Wisden* of 1985, which carried his obituary, Wellesley could have saved himself, but stood by, giving up his seat in the lifeboat to an elderly gentleman. It was a gesture that was typical of the man. Wellesley Fagge died as he'd lived, sticking to his lifelong belief that one should always give the opposition a better than even chance of winning – even when that opposition was the sea.

TERRY FRAMWELL

Bowls

Think of gypsy curses and haunted green glass eyes, and who is the first sportsman that springs to mind? Canoeist Jack Winstanley perhaps, or Malcolm 'Praise the Lord' Andrews? Certainly not Terry Framwell, for a brief while a legend in his native Cornwall, and without doubt the greatest one-legged bowls player this country has ever produced.

Neville Terrence Framwell was born in Launceston, Cornwall, in 1970. His father, George, ran a bakery business which had sewn up the market for hot cross buns in the north Cornwall area. Unfortunately for his family, George Framwell insisted that every bun had to be sold at either one a penny or two a penny, in strict accordance with the words of the nursery rhyme. For years they struggled, ironically, on the bread line, until a fateful day in June 1977. Following a complaint, the Framwell bakery was raided by food-safety inspectors, who discovered to their horror that the filling for one of the speciality pies was four and twenty blackbirds. When the pie was opened, the birds did not begin to sing as they'd all been roasted to death at gas mark 6. The bakery was closed, although not before the inspectors had expressed their appreciation of the intricate crimping on the pie crust.

Concerned that his parents might have been feeding him unsuitable food, and at reports that George was planning to build a house entirely made from gingerbread, young Terry was spirited away by social workers and sent to Downmarsh Hall, a local children's home. One of the more unusual aspects of Downmarsh Hall was its bowling green, an expanse of lawn that was immaculately maintained. As luck would have it, young Terry was a bowls natural. He'd shown a flair for the sport since the age of four, when he would roll stale Christmas puddings in his garden with uncanny accuracy. Terry soon made his mark in the world of junior Cornish bowls, and trophies, trinkets, plates, cups and baubles all started coming the way of the young baker boy. So great was his success that Downmarsh Hall had to build an extension to house all Terry's silverware. Sadly, a few months later it was pulled down because no one had applied for planning permission.

In 1978, aged only eight, Terry Framwell became the youngest ever winner of the Colonel Cootes-Harrington Memorial Cup, an enormous trophy awarded to the best young bowls player who came from a broken home. He won it again the following year and looked set for a wonderful future in the glittering world of bowls – until disaster struck, when he tragically lost a leg on a brass-rubbing trip. The miscreants and unfortunates of Downmarsh Hall had gone on a school journey to Truro and the excited youngsters had rushed into the cathedral with their paper, wax crayons and fish-paste sandwiches. Terry went his own way and proceeded to do a rubbing of the nearest railway line – with disastrous results. His left leg was chopped clean off and, what was worse, he got very poor marks for his brass rubbing.

A year later, when he'd fully recovered, Terry set to work fashioning himself an artificial limb, putting to good use all those hours he'd spent in the hospital metalwork shop. He collected all the cups and trophies that had been damaged when the extension was pulled down, and created a solid silver peg leg the likes of which had never been seen – certainly not in Cornwall. It was inspired by eighteenth-century Venetian casting techniques, although there was a slight hint of baroque about the design. All told, it wasn't bad for a ten-year-old boy.

After such a close run-in with the grim reaper, Terry Framwell's bowls comeback was keenly awaited. He duly made it in the summer of 1981 against the Junior Naughty Boys of Somerset. Disastrously for Terry, though his new leg looked very impressive, it was completely impractical. In the first end, against a troublemaker from Frome, Terry completely misjudged the sheer weight of metal on his left-hand side, and toppled over. Cornwall were trounced, five nothing. At one stage Miss Donovan, the Downmarsh Hall bowls coach, rushed on to give Terry some assistance but she was rudely brushed aside. One of bowls least-known rules states that if a player falls over he can't be helped to his feet. Or foot.

Terry tried to hollow out the leg for the following match, a cup tie against the Troublesome Teenagers of South-East Devon, but he overcompensated, and this time keeled over in the opposite direction.

Most young lads, faced with the loss of a limb, would probably have let their bowls game drift – maybe even given up the sport altogether. But Terry Framwell, metal leg aside, was not like other boys. For an eleven-year-old monopod, he was a sharp cookie, who reckoned that balance was the key to his success. Spending hours in the school workshop, he cast himself a splendid silver foot, and found that it worked wonders. In the Borstal Cup final against Witney's School for Misbehaving Children he proved unstoppable.

But while the governors at Downmarsh Hall were delighted at the recovery of their protégé, Terry Framwell's return was not to everybody's liking. Mr Simpkins, the Witney headmaster, objected to Terry's elaborately carved metal foot, which played havoc with the greens. When the boy ran after his bowl to check the line and length, his footsteps immediately rendered the surface unplayable. Throughout his rehabilitation Terry had been coached by his Uncle Alf, a plucky little fellow who'd seen active service in the Second World War. Alf had taught his nephew to lob the bowl over the rutted greens as though it was an assault weapon, and while the other boys struggled with the unplayable surface, Terry took it all in his stride. The critics howled, but there was nothing in the rulebook which forbade metal-footed boys, and young Terry quite reasonably just got on with his game. As a reward for their endeavours, each of the Downmarsh lads won their weight in tobacco, an unusual prize in 1981, when the dangers of smoking were well known. The school doctor promptly confiscated most of the tobacco for himself, only allowing the boys to keep a token ten kilogrammes each for themselves.

In 1985 Terry Framwell found himself suspended by the snobbish Junior Bowls Association (Miscreants Division), who stressed that their decision was in no way personal.

They'd uncovered an old rule that said that any boy who was considered a fire risk could be barred from the game, and Terry Framwell, they argued, was a lightning hazard. Downmarsh Hall pleaded with the authorities to change their mind and, when that didn't work, ordered Terry to replace his silver leg with a wooden one, ideally without a clawed foot. The boy refused. Even his father, now serving a life sentence, tried to make Terry see sense. He sent his son an enormous fruit cake, inside of which were a file and a note telling him to smooth the rough edges of his metallic foot. It's perhaps the only occasion on which a file has been smuggled out of prison.

Six months later, the Association's decision was academic anyway. As he turned sixteen, Terry Framwell qualified as a senior bowler, where different rules applied. In the adult game no one cared whether a bowls player had feet made of wood, metal, plastic, flesh or had no feet whatsoever. He made his eagerly awaited senior debut – and indeed final appearance – in the Gloucestershire Open of 1986. Tournament officials watched nervously as Terry, lobbing brilliantly, ripped the manicured greens to shreds. The teenager won the final by a record score over Mr Wallington, by no means a bowls slouch, on a green that looked more like a ploughed field.

A week later the British Bowls Confederation changed the rules and Terry Framwell was expelled. It was nothing to do with the dangers of lightning, they assured him, but altogether more technical. From now on the bowl would have to stay in contact with the ground at all times, and could no longer be lobbed. Not surprisingly, young Terry called it quits soon after that, and the bowls world never heard from him again. He was just sixteen years old.

In 1988 Terry moved to Coleraine in Northern Ireland where he bought a market garden with the proceeds of all the metal he'd hollowed out from his first silver leg. The following summer, on a trip to buy manure, he met Christine, the heir to the Vaughan Fertilizer fortune, and within a matter of weeks the pair were preparing to get married. Before the happy day, however, Terry Framwell was struck by lightning and killed in a flash. He foolishly clambered on to the roof of his greenhouse in a thunderstorm, tried to dislodge a wasps' nest from the eaves with his artificial limb, and was burnt to a crisp. After his proper cremation, Christine held a bowls match in her fiancé's honour, using only the very best cabbages, grown by Terry. It was a fitting tribute to the greatest bowls-playing teenager that Great Britain has ever produced.

LUCINDA KILGOUR

Rowing

No one knew the rules of any game better than Lucinda Kilgour. It was she who first spotted the anomaly in the rules of conkers which permitted the use of non-horse chestnuts in certain circumstances. Even at the age of eight she knew every wrinkle in the rulebook, and her concrete conker smashed all opposition in the playground until it retired as an undefeated four hundred and thirty-sixer. By the time that particular oversight in the rules had been changed 'Loophole Lu', as she became known, had moved on to other things.

Lucinda Clark Kilgour was born in Dundee in the sweltering hot summer of 1976, when Scotland enjoyed a record five days of unbroken sunshine. Lucinda's parents both worked in the local jute factory, making rope. Jute manufacture is well known for its side effects, which can induce acute recklessness and selfishness, particularly in very pale-skinned people. Mr Kilgour was an extremely pallid man with a luxuriant head of ginger hair, qualities his precious daughter inherited. At the age of four she was crowned Scotland's Most Freckled Wee Lassie – a most prestigious competition – which she won with a record

FORGOTTEN SPORTING HEROES No. 30

LUCINDA KILGOUR

ROWING

freckle count of more than sixty per square inch. Only when she was a little older did Lucinda become aware that her father had been responsible for her surfeit of freckles. Fearing a repeat triumph by little Maggie McGregor, the Melanoma Maid of Strathclyde, Mr Kilgour had dosed his daughter with large quantities of polychromal bromide, a chemical used in the dyeing of jute. Lucinda had promptly broken out in an incredible facial rash, which had lasted long enough for her to claim the cup.

Whether this early success had an effect on young Lucinda's personality has been fiercely debated by Scottish psychologists ever since, although they are all agreed that it did. By the age of nine, with her freckle and conker triumphs behind her, Lucinda Kilgour had clearly caught the competitive bug, and was not prepared to accept second place in anything. Exam results, as well as sports competitions were pored over in the minutest detail, and anyone who dared to beat her would invariably find themselves penalized or disqualified for the tiniest of infractions. In 1985 Lucinda managed to have the Dundee area junior skipping champion, the brilliant Wee Wendy Patterson, disqualified on the grounds that she had skipped to an inappropriate rhyme. Her skipping doggerel . . .

Mary McGonagall
Said the Evening Chronicle
Dropped her daughter
In a pail of water.
The little girl drowned
A note was found
Saying Mary McGonagall
Had run away to Donegal.

. . . contravened the rules. Donegal was in Ireland, argued Lucinda, which meant that Wee Wendy's rhyme was insufficiently Scottish. The judges reluctantly agreed, and Lucinda Kilgour was declared the champion.

The results of a hopscotch tournament were also over-turned in Lucinda's favour, while several rival girls found themselves disqualified from a spelling contest for chewing their pencils in a way that might cause distress to fellow competitors. The swimming pool, which she had never been able to master, was filled with concrete as a safety precaution.

By the age of twelve, nobody at St Murdo's School would speak to Lucinda, but it didn't seem to matter to her. She consoled herself with the cups and rosettes which filled her bedroom. Had there been a trophy for the most spoiled girl in Scotland, Lucinda Kilgour would surely have won it unopposed. As it was, her father made one for her, and filled it to overflowing with sweets and teddies.

In 1991, concerned that Lucinda might not pass her Scottish Higher exams – and how she might react when she found out – Mr Kilgour withdrew her from St Murdo's. He rented an abandoned lighthouse on the uninhabited island of Gloch, in the Firth of Argyll, and home-educated – or rather lighthouse-educated – his daughter. Over the next two years she passed every single exam set by the hastily formed Gloch Education Board, never scoring less than one hundred per cent.

Since her triumphs in skipping and hopscotch, Lucinda had shown very little interest in sport, but that all changed in July 1992. It was the summer of the Barcelona Olympics, and in the lonely lighthouse Lucinda fell in love with the Games, and pestered her father to get her an Olympic gold medal. Far away from the factory, and with his mind no longer befuddled by jute, Mr Kilgour tried to explain that becoming an Olympic champion was no easy task, and that it would require years of hard work and dedication. When Lucinda finally stopped her hysterical screaming – about a week later – he promised he would get her one.

The standard of women's rowing didn't look especially high, he declared, so for the next three years Lucinda familiarized herself with the tenets of the sport. Occasionally she would row round the lighthouse, but more often she would study the rules of rowing, looking for the tiniest possible loophole that would boost her chances. By the summer of 1995 the pair of them had found one, and began designing a rowing boat that would conquer the world.

To gain selection to the British Olympic team for 1996, Lucinda first had to win a trial race, so she demanded that she be allowed to try out her boat at the snooty Henley Rowing Regatta. The committee were nonplussed – apart from Steve Redgrave they had never had an entrant before who wasn't hoity toity or a southerner, but when Lucinda pointed out there was nothing in the rules which prevented Scottish rowers from competing, they eventually relented.

When they saw her boat lining up at the start of the race, the blazered Henley officials were aghast. No one had ever turned up in a home-made boat before – least of all one that was 380 metres long. Lucinda reminded them that according to the statutes, there was nothing that specified the maximum length of a boat, and she clambered into her seat, which was halfway towards the finishing line. Unfortunately for the spoiled Scottish girl, although the boat was very long, it was also very fragile, and she managed no more than two strokes of the oars before the craft, made of Peruvian balsa wood, began to crack and splinter. As the other rowers raced by, Lucinda floundered and, unable to swim, soon sank below the surface.

A few onlookers, distressed at the sight, suggested diving in to rescue the girl, but were prevented from doing so by the course steward. He reminded them of the recently discovered technical loophole which prevented anybody from diving into the Thames to rescue a ginger person on a Tuesday. Lucinda Kilgour's body was never recovered.

When they heard the news at St Murdo's, the children made a new skipping rhyme in the playground, which they sing to this day.

> Lucinda Kilgour
> Lived in a big tower
> She made herself a long boat
> But it wouldn't stay afloat
> Her dad was distraughter
> When she fell into the water
> What a tasty dish
> For the River Thames fish.

GEOFFREY OF BROMSGROVE

Archery

Britain's first true sporting superstar is almost forgotten nowadays, but in his day – the 1460s – he was a household name, whether that house was a hovel, a farm, a castle or a rudimentary wattle-and-daub construction. It's a great pity no one remembers him because, in all honesty, Geoffrey of Bromsgrove deserves to be lauded as England's finest archer – better than Robin Hood, who is of course a fictional character, and William Tell, who actually came from Switzerland.

Geoffrey was born in the Worcestershire village of Bromsgrove around 1438. We don't know the exact date, nor the name of his parents. Surnames were in short supply in the fifteenth century, and first names frequently displayed a distinct lack of imagination. There are no written records of his early years, and Geoffrey himself wasn't entirely helpful in providing the details. When he became famous he spoke very little about his upbringing – on various occasions saying he had been a peasant farmer, a pargeter, a pewterer, a cooper, a polecat skinner or a weaver, depending on which pretty maiden he was trying to impress. What is indisputable is that Geoffrey of Bromsgrove was a first-class archer.

In the mid-fifteenth century it was compulsory for all free men of England to practise their skills with a longbow, and Geoffrey would have been one of thousands firing arrows at a target during his time off from farming, pargeting, pewtering, coopering, skinning polecats, weaving or whatever it was he did for a living. If his tales to the fair Margaret of Potters Bar are true, then he saw action at the ill-fated Battle of Castillon in 1453, when the English finally lost their last remaining provinces in France. During this rearguard action – which brought the Hundred Years War to a premature close – Geoffrey claimed to have killed no less than a dozen Frenchmen, an impressive total for an archer aged only fifteen.

The oldest surviving documentary evidence of Geoffrey of Bromsgrove occurs in the County Rolls of Essex for 1458. He is listed as a competitor in the Great Dunmow Games, where he won a haunch of venison and a handkerchief belonging to the fair Margaret of Cockfosters. The great troubadour, Geoffrey of Tewkesbury, composed a madrigal in his honour, but unfortunately that has been lost to posterity.

In 1460 Geoffrey was crowned champion archer of Nottinghamshire – a county famous for its bowmen – when he eventually outscored Geoffrey of Leicester after a gruelling contest. It climaxed, literally, in a sudden death play-off, in which poor Geoffrey of Leicester paid with his life. A few months later, in the summer of 1461, Geoffrey of Bromsgrove was one of the star turns at the Wells Festival, a celebration of archery, jousting, synchronized falconry, music and culinary delights. In the days before mass communication, when printing was in its infancy, word of Geoffrey's participation travelled fast. Serfs, peasants, free-men and women, not to mention nobles and clergymen, queued in their thousands to buy advance tickets. Those that could afford the two groat entry fee were not dis-appointed. Geoffrey won the top prize, the Bishop of Bath and Wells Chalice, when he shot three arrows through a lacy doily without damaging the fabric. In addition to the chalice, Geoffrey also won a night in the bedchamber of the fair Margaret of Taunton, an unofficial prize he nevertheless readily accepted. While Geoffrey's exploits are largely forgotten, the Wells Festival is best remembered now for the invention of ice cream when medieval England's finest culinary genius, Geoffrey of Portsmouth, filled an upturned lady's wimple with fruit-flavoured ice. The impractically large treat proved unpopular – not least because it ruined wimples – and was destined not to catch on for another 500 years until the invention of the wafer cornet.

In 1462 England resumed its perennial fight with the French, and thousands of archers were shipped over to Calais, the country's last remaining foothold in France. Geoffrey of Bromsgrove was not among them. His sup-porters denied that his reluctance to fight was down to cowardice, and insisted that it was because he'd been hideously cursed by a jealous archery rival. Although nobody had seen them there were reports that Geoffrey had sprouted antlers, and had needed to disappear on a secret pilgrimage to Spain to get rid of them. Only when the fight-ing in Calais had finished did Geoffrey re-emerge, his antlers gone and the scars miraculously healed over completely.

Geoffrey's next competition was the Norwich Pig-Sticking Tourney of 1464. He duly won the archery contest, which restored the event's reputation. The previous year's winner, Geoffrey of Bury St Edmunds, had been disqualified when he tested positive for excessive quantities of eye of newt.

All sport was cancelled by royal proclamation in 1465 owing to an outbreak of bubonic plague, so archery fans had to wait until 1466 for the contest everyone was waiting for – the Stoke Poges Games. Not only would Geoffrey of Bromsgrove be competing, but so would the other two best archers in the land – Geoffrey of Haywards Heath, and another Geoffrey of Bromsgrove, known to his supporters as The Other Geoffrey of Bromsgrove. (It should be pointed out that the 1460s was a decade which experienced a surfeit of Geoffreys.)

Before the contest, there was much verbal sparring. Geoffrey of Bromsgrove, dressed in his favourite red and green doublet and hose, declared that he could defeat the other two Geoffreys with one hand tied behind his back – a foolish claim which would have seriously hampered his archery. Geoffrey of Haywards Heath angrily retorted that he should go back to his guild, the Worshipful Company of Boasters.

But cometh the hour Geoffrey of Bromsgrove was as good as his word. He dazzled the crowd with a stunning array of trick shots – over his shoulder, through his legs, over a gentleman's shoulder and through a lady's legs – leaving the two other Geoffreys to fight for scraps. By the end of the contest he'd claimed the first prize – the hand of the fair Margaret of Stoke Poges in marriage. (There was a similar glut of Margarets in the 1460s.) He was also presented with a velvet bag of beans, which the local alchemist assured him were magic and would transform into pure gold the minute he got them home.

We can only speculate whether Geoffrey's prize did transform itself from base beans to gold, although a basic understanding of the laws of chemistry tells us it's impossible. What we know for certain is that at the next archery tournament, the Winchester Open of 1467, Geoffrey of Bromsgrove died. After effortlessly winning the tournament he signed a few autographs for admirers, but then – perhaps intoxicated by his success or the powerful Winchester ale – he foolishly accepted a challenge that cost him his life. A linnet was singing its heart out on top of the nearby cathedral. A small boy – possibly named Geoffrey – asked the champion archer if he could shoot the bird with his bow and arrow. He could shoot it through the heart, Geoffrey of Bromsgrove informed the crowd of onlookers, and what was more, if he missed, they could chop him in half with a sword. The bird flew away just as he shot.

Geoffrey of Bromsgrove is buried in Winchester and Eastleigh.

SISTER AGNES BROWN

Rugby Union

If they handed out medals for niceness, then Sister Agnes Brown – Ursuline nun, friend of the unfortunate, and one of the greatest rugby coaches the game has ever seen – would surely be at the head of the queue. Although being so nice, no doubt she would have ushered someone else forward and said, 'No, you go first.' For that was her nature.

Agnes Brown first breathed life in 1899, in the Scottish border town of Selkirk. She lived with her mother Eileen and her Uncle Donald, a brutish man with a quick temper and surprisingly delicate hands for a shopkeeper. No one ever knew what happened to Agnes's biological father, although for many years there was malicious gossip in the pubs and clubs of Selkirk – mainly concerning Uncle Donald's volatile temper and a suspicious mound in the back garden.

Agnes's education was modest, to say the least. She showed little enthusiasm or aptitude for Latin, Scottish Maths and Scottish History – nor even for traditional girls' disciplines like Embroidery and Tidying-Up. But while she wasn't academically gifted, Agnes had a kind heart and could frequently be found on the streets of Selkirk, standing

FORGOTTEN SPORTING HEROES No. 32

SISTER AGNES BROWN
RUGBY UNION

outside the pubs saying endless prayers for the lost. Her uncle did attempt to beat some sense into the girl, but this only had the curious effect of making Agnes more determined to be good.

The only official activity at which Agnes showed any proficiency was rugby – then, as now, hugely popular in the Scottish border region. By the time she'd turned fourteen she was captain of her school and had trials with Selkirkshire Under-fifteens.

It was only a matter of time before young Agnes came to the attention of the local nuns. Her natural talent and spirit of Christian charity made her an obvious candidate for the cloistered life – more importantly though, she was a genius with a rugby ball. It's a little known fact that rugby is hugely popular amongst Britain's nunneries. The sport is seen as a metaphor for Christianity, with all its talk of conversions, tight-head scrimmaging and annual matches against the Barbarians.

In 1915, with Britain at war, and with plenty of better offers from rival nunneries – Agnes surprisingly threw in her lot with the Ursuline Convent at Tweedsmuir, a tiny village just off the A701. Tweedsmuir had known better days – specifically in 1803 when Sir Walter Scott had paid a fleeting visit – and in 1915 it was in the doldrums. But the Mother Superior had bold plans for the nunnery, which she hoped could have the best rugby team in the region.

Hopeless at learning huge swathes of the Bible, Agnes, the young novice, was instead encouraged to spend her time on the training ground. Her talent soon had a galvanizing effect on the other nuns, and by the end of the season they'd surprised themselves and the world of Scottish monastic rugby by winning the Selkirkshire Cup. The following season Tweedsmuir won promotion to the top division of convent rugby.

Melrose Abbey was the powerhouse of Scottish nun-based sport. Founded in 1136, the great institution had swept all before it for more than two decades. Now, at last, Melrose had a rival worthy of the name. In 1921, for the first time, the Abbey and Tweedsmuir met one another on a level playing field – with just a marginal slope and a few divots and potholes here and there. Under Sister Agnes's leadership the nuns of Tweedsmuir went on the attack from the first whistle, and soon built up a formidable lead. Not even the presence of some nuns with suspicious New Zealand and South African accents in the Melrose side could affect the outcome, and at the end of the game Sister Agnes was chaired from the field in triumph, as Tweedsmuir prevailed by twenty-four points to six.

By 1924, it seemed as if Agnes had the rugby world at her feet. A profile of her had appeared in the *Peebles Echo*, and the Governor-General of Barbados – a man who was an expert on monastic sport – had crossed the Atlantic to watch her play. But on a bitterly cold January afternoon, in a championship decider against Melrose, disaster struck. With Tweedsmuir holding a fourteen point lead, thanks in no small part to her two tries, Sister Agnes left the pitch, complaining of stomach cramps. In her absence the team lost its way and conceded twenty points and victory in the last few minutes. Suspicion immediately fell on Sister Agnes's half-time gruel. Had it been tampered with? No one could say. Sister Mildred had washed the bowl, and all the evidence had gone down the plughole.

Try as she might, and despite the countless prayers people made for her recovery, Sister Agnes never played rugby again. At the ripe old age of twenty-five, her days on the park were all over. But it was far from the end of her rugby life. The Mother Superior sacked the team coach and appointed Sister Agnes in his place. Although desperately weak, and on an intravenous drip of loaves and fishes, she was soon out on the training ground again putting the sisters through their paces. Her new regime worked wonders – in particular the purchase of a scrum machine and some extra-cold showers.

If anything, the nuns of Tweedsmuir were an even better outfit with Sister Agnes masterminding the play from the touchlines. For the next two seasons the convent won every game before it, becoming rightly famous for its expansive playing style, its innovative use of overlapping backs and for Sister Polly, the well-endowed second row forward.

Then, in 1928, came a bolt from the blue. A steel bolt, in fact, which had somehow dislodged itself from the chapel guttering and tragically brained Sister Polly, who happened to be doing some light weeding in the garden below. Worse was to follow – fond though everyone was of Sister Polly. A representative arrived from the Scottish Rugby Football Union, a Mr Harris, who accused Sister Agnes of gross improprieties and conduct inconsistent with the game. The Tweedsmuir coach, he claimed, was a professional rugby player. Mr Harris offered copper-bottomed proof that Sister Agnes had received payment for playing – namely, a sixpenny piece left on a collecting plate after a match with Kelso in 1923. It was irrelevant that the sixpence in question had been used to buy mutton soup for the destitute of Peeblesshire. Money was money, and it made her a professional – and rugby union did not countenance professionalism.

Protestations of innocence weren't allowed in those days – especially not by nuns – and Sister Agnes Brown never coached rugby again. There were a couple of offers – from the rugby-league playing convents of Warrington and St Helens – but they came to nothing.

Agnes spent her remaining years – and there were a lot of them – in quiet retirement. She tended the herb garden, and occasionally skinned the odd seal to make a sou'wester, until she passed away in 1982.

The nuns of Tweedsmuir rarely talk about their illustrious predecessor, but they have no need. Above the door in the great hall is a huge tapestry, embroidered by Sister Agnes herself, showing the nunnery winning the cup in 1921. It's an impressive reminder of the greatest rugby-playing nun who ever lived.

GIDEON HALFBRASS

Weightlifting

There's no doubting who has the distinction of being Britain's most pampered athlete. Gideon Halfbrass, true to form, did not turn up to collect his reward – the Fluffy Golden Pillow of Southport – but that was understandable. His mum had sent him to bed with a bad cold.

Gideon Halfbrass was born in Leeds in 1962, shortly before the outbreak of Beatlemania. He was, by turn, cosseted, mollycoddled, overindulged and at all times wrapped in cotton wool by his mother, Hilda Halfbrass. It can't have been easy for young Gideon, walking to school holding his mother's hand – especially when he reached fifteen and still had pads strapped to his knees in case he fell over and hurt himself. But if he was embarrassed, Gideon bore it with typical Yorkshire stoicism. He was a large boy, with a very fierce mother, and it was a rare child indeed who tried to tease Gideon Halfbrass more than once.

If he seems like an unlikely sportsman, that's because he was. His sporting prowess – his titanic strength – was first manifested when he was six years old. While his mother fretted that her little cherub wouldn't come to any harm,

Gideon single-handedly hoisted a bookcase off the floor so that his teacher, Miss Fairbairn, might rescue the class gerbil which had scurried underneath it. When she heard what had happened Mrs Halfbrass had a fainting fit – although not before she'd taken Gideon home, where he remained for the next fortnight.

The Leeds area boasted a competitive under-eights weightlifting league, and Gideon's headmaster, Mr Scobey, was keen for the boy to join the team. Hilda Halfbrass would hear nothing of it – neither then, nor in the remaining four years Gideon spent at junior school. Whenever a competition was scheduled, the boy would brandish a note from his mother which usually explained that on account of him having a dicky tummy, or being a bit peaky, he would be unable to lift weights. Years later these notes were all collected together in a leather-bound volume, but that's another story.

News of Gideon's Herculean strength preceded him to secondary school, where his headmaster – also called Mr Scobey but completely unrelated to the other one – attempted to get him into the weightlifting club. But he fared no better. Chilblains was the most frequent excuse that Gideon's letter outlined – even during the summer months – but every single week, without fail, he was under the weather and couldn't compete. Then, miraculously, one day Gideon either forgot his note or was completely fit and well. But either, way, deprived of an excuse not to compete, Mr Scobey frogmarched the boy off to the school weight-lifting room. He'd just rubbed some chalk on his hands and was preparing his first lift when Mrs Halfbrass rushed shrieking into the gym, mumbled something about a runny nose and dragged Gideon off the stage.

Thwarted on that occasion, Mr Scobey persisted. He entered Gideon for the All Yorkshire Schools Weightlifting Championships, to be held that year in Richmond. Reluctantly, Mrs Halfbrass gave consent for her son to compete. She packed his singlet and shorts, made him a flask of hot, weak tea and some cheese and pickle sandwiches, then bade him a tearful farewell from Leeds railway station. Tragically, Gideon Halfbrass never got to compete. Owing to an administrative error, the All Yorkshire Schools Weightlifting Championships were switched at the last minute to Richmond in Surrey, rather than North Yorkshire, and none of the cups were claimed.

In the early 1980s, when Gideon Halfbrass left school, British competitive weightlifting was in a wretched state. British lifters consistently failed to medal at any of the major events, and Louis Martin's bronze in 1964 had been the last success at Olympic level. For twenty years or more Eastern European nations had gobbled up the weightlifting medals. Then, in 1984, came the news that set British weightlifting pulses racing. The Russians and their Communist allies were going to boycott the forthcoming Los Angeles Olympics. The chances of winning a medal – of any colour – were better than they ever had been. Grown men with ridiculously big muscles and over-veined necks ran from their gyms and danced in the streets.

A deputation was despatched from British weightlifting headquarters up to Leeds, to persuade Mrs Halfbrass to let her son compete in the games. Although he was twenty-two, Gideon still lived at home where his mother could keep a protective eye on him. Try as they might to persuade Hilda Halfbrass to let her son compete in Los Angeles, it took her less than three minutes to send them packing. Gideon couldn't possibly go to America, Hilda explained. If he went by sea he'd get an upset stomach, and flying would only make his ears go pop. In the circumstances, she concluded, it would be much better if Gideon stayed in Leeds. As it turned out, he did just that. Deprived of his presence, the team of British weightlifters returned empty-handed from the Los Angeles Olympics.

There are rumours that a splinter group from the British Weightlifting Federation did consider kidnapping Gideon Halfbrass, bundling him on a plane, taking him to Los Angeles and making him compete. Although the claim has been consistently denied, it is a story that has refused to go away. Yet while Mrs Hilda Halfbrass watched over her son day and night, who would dare to incur her wrath by spiriting him away? It's true that he might have stood a chance of winning a gold medal, but it was a risk that no one in British weightlifting was prepared to take.

Gideon Halfbrass still lives at home with his mother.

DILSHAN HARPOT

Twig Fondlin'

Over the years our American cousins have been responsible for some inventive – one might even say ridiculous – sports. Melon-seed spitting, hub-cap throwing, bobbing for pig's feet, American football and monster-truck racing are just a few that have originated on the other side of the Atlantic. Most of the time we ignore these pursuits, but in 1996 our attention was gripped when the Olympic Games featured another North American sport – twig fondlin'.

Twig fondlin' – described by its adherents as a no-nonsense outdoor activity – involves recognizing species of trees merely by stroking them. As a sport it lacks the obvious visual excitement of cycling, shinty, water polo or football, but it's certainly competitive and in many respects highly dangerous.

It's the right of every Olympic host city to include a demonstration sport for consideration at future games. As the hosts for 1996, the American city of Atlanta chose a sport that was little known outside Georgia, never mind the United States, but their dogged persistence paid off when twig fondlin' was given the Olympic nod ahead of mud-pit belly flopping and included on the programme. The news stunned almost the entire world, with the possible exception of two men from Dover, Bill and Ronald Kaplan, the United Kingdom's foremost twig fondlers. Unfortunately, at the time of the announcement neither man was on speaking terms with the other, each having formed rival twig fondlin' organizations which claimed to represent the sport. Ronald Kaplan was the co-founder, and by 1996 the sole member, of TFCUK, the Twig Fondlin' Confederation of the United Kingdom. His brother Bill, meanwhile, had established the rival TITSBAB, the Tactile Identification of Twigs and Small Branches Association of Britain, following an argument with Ronald over the size of his name on the letter heading. With only one place allocated for each nation, the choice was hopelessly deadlocked between the two Kaplan brothers, each of whom proved as intractable as the mighty oak they'd fondled so many times before. As the time ticked down to Atlanta, CRISPYDUK, the Council for Recreation, Integrated Sport and Pastimes (Youth Development) UK, agonized over which of the brothers, if any, to send to the Games.

It was lucky, then, that another talent should emerge, who could carry the flag and fondle the twigs for Great Britain. Dilshan Harpot, a bespectacled young man who worked in the Green Fingers Arboretum on the outskirts of Bedford, had quite a reputation amongst his colleagues. After the hurricane of 1987, he'd put back all the identification labels which had been blown off on to their correct trees. He'd also received a commendation for his work with the blind, a greater part of which involved getting them to fondle and stroke the trees in the Green Fingers collection. By the time they went home, most sightless visitors could tell an ash from a hornbeam – even in winter – merely by rubbing their fingers along the twigs.

Dilshan's emergence naturally caused problems for the Kaplans, both of whom thought they should be given the nod. Neither, though, would stand aside to allow the other to compete. The boys' mother, old Mrs Kaplan, tried to knock some sense into them, but only ended up trying too hard. Bill lost several teeth, while Ronald was severely concussed and missed a few days' work at the goose-rendering factory. By the time both had fully recovered, Dilshan Harpot had been selected.

The Arboretum was generous enough to let Dilshan train during company time, and for an hour or so each day he'd jog, lift weights and fondle twigs to his heart's content. CRISPYDUK even supplied him with a coach, Tommy O'Riordan, to help him prepare. Tommy had trained several Olympic-level athletes in the past, and while he didn't know the first thing about arboriculture, he was wise enough to recognize that on home turf the American twig fondler would have an advantage. So, after his morning aerobics, he'd send Dilshan to practise his digital dexterity in the American plant house, where he could familiarize himself with some of the North American twigs he was likely to have to identify.

Dilshan travelled to Atlanta in good spirits. His training had gone well and the calluses on his fingers, caused when he'd rubbed some Turkey oak bark too vigorously, had healed. He was, he informed a reporter from the *Bedfordshire Argus*, in the twig fondlin' form of his life.

Deprived of official status, there was only the most subdued ballyhoo in the Martin Luther King Twig Fondlin' Arena when the event took place. Apart from the

Bedfordshire Argus, the only British representative in the press box came from *Gardener's World* magazine. Athletes from no less than twenty-eight of the world's tree-loving nations assembled to compete. There was Eric Knudsen, the wily Norwegian; Pierre Duhamel, known in his native France as 'Le Roi des Ramilles', literally 'the King of Twigs'; Wilhelm Vogt, the German tree fanatic was there too, as was Australia's Jeff Jackson, the self-styled 'Fondler from Down Under'. Gossip on the twig fondlin' grapevine gave Dilshan Harpot an outside chance, but the overwhelming favourite was the local man, Sanders Redmond. He was a burly-looking man, with tattoos of his favourite twigs the length and breadth of his enormous arms.

For more than two-and-a-half hours (excluding a ten-minute coffee break) the competitors sat blindfolded alongside a conveyor belt, picking up twigs, rubbing them and yelling out their names, while 3,000 spectators watched their every fondle. By the half-way mark Dilshan and Sanders Redmond were jointly in the lead – Dilshan matching his American rival twig for twig. Of the other contenders, only an outsider, Luxembourg's Gaston Pleussy, had threatened them. For a while it seemed as though the Grand Duchy might have a shot at a rare Olympic medal, until Pleussy jabbed his finger on one of the thorns of the poisonous *Quillobarbus,* the Texan brush pine, and by the coffee break he'd lapsed into a paralysis from which he has yet to recover.

Once the ambulance had departed and the coffee had been drunk, the second half resumed. It was then that Dilshan Harpot's rigorous training – all the running up sand dunes, the weights in the gym, the hours on his hands and knees in the Green Fingers shrubbery – paid off. Redmond, corpulent and physically unfit, began to sweat under the lights. After more than two hours of fondlin' he made his first misidentification when he confused a *Sorbus* for an *Abutilon*. The crowd – not all of them tree experts by any means – gasped in shock. At Olympic-level twig fondlin' it was a basic error. Five minutes later Redmond miscalled another twig and the contest was effectively over. Britain's Dilshan Harpot was the demonstration gold medal winner.

Despite being the overwhelming favourite, Sanders Redmond was gracious in defeat and admitted he'd been out-fondled by the better man. He nevertheless vowed to take his revenge in four years time at the Sydney Olympics.

Although his success was largely overlooked by the British media, Dilshan Harpot was fêted in his native Bedford. He was given an open-topped bus tour of the town – a generous gesture which sadly backfired. Heading out to the Green Fingers Arboretum, and while Dilshan was waving at well wishers, the bus passed under a low hanging sycamore tree. He failed to notice it until it was too late, with the result that he was lacerated across the eyes by the branches. For a time it was thought that Dilshan would pay with his sight, and for a few weeks he could be seen working in the Arboretum with bandages over his eyes, but in the end they got better, while a tree surgeon saw to the troublesome sycamore.

The IOC decided not to adopt twig fondlin' as a full Olympic sport, so the much anticipated rematch between Dislhan Harpot and Sanders Redmond has never happened. Nor is it likely. Dilshan is now the general manager at Green Fingers, and having full responsibility for the running of the arboretum leaves him no free time for competitive twig fondlin'.

The latest reports indicate that Bill and Ronald Kaplan are still not on speaking terms.

SIR PERCIVAL NEAME, 'SCRAPPER' WATKINS, ALFIE 'THE GRUB' BROWNE AND OTHERS

Sir Percival Neame's Obstacle Race for Urchins

Doggett's Coat and Badge is a rowing race which takes place each year between apprentice watermen on the River Thames. First held in 1715, it is believed to be the oldest sporting event in continued existence. Almost as old, but much less well known, is Sir Percival Neame's Obstacle Race for Urchins, a hugely demanding contest which saw its fair share of pain, heartache, triumph, tragedy, stolen fruit, raw sewage and some of the cheekiest competitors who ever drew breath.

Sir Percival Neame, the Assistant Commissioner of the Royal Exchange, established the race in 1724. Unlike many of his contemporaries, Neame had made a small fortune from the South Sea Company, trading in his shares at the height of their value before the bubble famously burst, causing countless bankruptcies and ruining reputations. His deputy, Sir Edmund Jukes, had lost everything in the crash and had resorted to begging, his upturned periwig at his

FORGOTTEN SPORTING HEROES No. 35

Sir PERCIVAL NEAME, 'SCRAPPER' WATKINS, ALFIE 'THE GRUB' BROWNE and others
Sir PERCIVAL NEAME'S OBSTACLE RACE FOR URCHINS

feet. Somewhat shamed by the straitened circumstances of his former colleague – not least because he'd sold him his shares – Neame devised a scheme that would not only give something back to the community, but might provide him and his friends with some amusement. Other philanthropists had endowed workhouses or charitable foundations – Sir Percival Neame decided to instigate an obstacle race for urchins.

London had no shortage of street urchins in 1724 – Thomas Hedley's *Librum Urchinarium* put the number at around 30,000. They could be seen pushing barrows, loitering near inns, gathering refuse and whistling, and might occasionally be spotted trying to steal a pie that had been left on a windowsill to cool. Barefoot and ragged-trousered children were also to be found scavenging on the banks of the Thames at low tide, although technically they were defined as mudlarks rather than urchins. Either way, Sir Percival Neame had no time for them.

In fact, it was the many facets of urchindom that had given Neame his idea. He wondered if there might not be some way to determine which was the best of them, and crown one of them king for the day. So, he devised a multi-part contest, which comprised pushing a barrow over cobbles without spilling any apples, climbing vertically up the inside of a fifty-foot chimney, going three times round Clerkenwell cesspit, then running back to Tower Bridge. The winner would receive a freshly minted sovereign and a pair of velvet breeches, which he was to wear while smoking a pipe full of tobacco and walking around the City of London until he was sick.

The first contest was won by little 'Arry Walker, a twelve-year-old guttersnipe from Whitechapel who was described by the *Spectator* as 'the best of London's barefoot scoundrels'.

Such had been the interest that the competition had attracted no less than 8,000 entrants, and Charing Cross Road – the starting point – had been completely choked. Sir Percival found himself reprimanded by the Lord Mayor of London, who warned him that the competition would need to be streamlined. If it wasn't it would bring anarchy and mayhem to the streets of London – neither of which things the Lord Mayor wanted – and Sir Percival would find himself thrown into Newgate Prison. Having no desire to swap his comfortable existence for a jail cell, Sir Percival agreed. In future, each urchin would need to provide a genuine certificate of urchinhood, together with proof that he lived on the streets within smelling distance of the River Thames, which was about a mile in each direction. The certificates proved so difficult to obtain that only fifteen urchins lined up to compete in 1725.

Despite the lower turn out, Sir Percival Neame's Obstacle Race for Urchins became an important event in the London calendar. It became quite fashionable for the city's elite to watch the races, and huge sums of money were often wagered on the outcome. The composer Handel won five guineas when 'Boot Black' Bob Richards won the competition in 1734, after which he went home and wrote his famous *Scruff's Oratorio*.

The Obstacle Race for Urchins continued each year 'on the second Tuesday after Michaelmas' until the death of Sir Percival Neame in 1761. Fortunately for London's urchins he had left a will, bequeathing enough money to supply gold sovereigns, velvet breeches and pipe tobacco to last another hundred years.

The changing nature of London, and of course its raggedy street-dwelling poor, meant that the rules of the Obstacle Race changed to suit the times. After the Act of Parliament which banned open cesspits from central London new challenges were introduced. These involved scrambling 100 yards down a sewage pipe, kicking a peeler in the shins and running off down Chancery Lane. Pipe-smoking was no longer quite so fashionable, so instead of a churchwarden full of tobacco the triumphant urchin was given a big fat cigar to smoke until he vomited.

The 1840s were perhaps the golden age for Sir Percival Neame's Obstacle Race for Urchins. It was even mentioned in Dickens's *David Copperfield*:

'I've been a watchin' the rapscallions' obstacle race, Mr Blatherchope. I won me a whole shillin' on that "Nobbler" Johnson.'
'A tidy sum, Mr Barkis, a tidy sum.'

The decade also saw one of the great rivalries of Victorian sport. Between 1840 and 1848, two notorious urchins – 'Scrapper' Watkins and Alfie 'The Grub' Browne – won the competition no less than four times each. 'Scrapper' Watkins, in 1845, became the first ragamuffin to win the event three years running. He was well known for his combination of cheeky Cockney demeanour and powerful leg muscles – extremely important when pushing the barrow or traversing the sewage pipe. His home, such as it was, consisted of a doorway near the Bank of England and was one of the more popular city landmarks visited by tourists. No one could mistake him, or the four pairs of neatly folded velvet breeches in various states of distress.

Alfie 'The Grub' Browne was more of a tactician – perhaps the first in the sport – always keeping back something for that last desperate sprint to London Bridge. When he retired, as a rather decrepit thirty-year-old urchin in 1860, he left behind a legacy. He opened a school for the training of street kids, complete with an authentic cobbled area, a sewage tunnel and an array of ropes and climbing frames. There were no sleeping quarters because to have provided a roof would have meant the children were no longer officially urchins, and thus disqualified from the event. It proved to be a success and no less than fourteen future champions came from Alfie's ragged school.

As well as great rivalries, there were controversial moments too. In 1822, 'Wriggler' Wilson disappeared when he scrambled up a chimney breast and was never seen again; in 1855, 'Fruity Boy' Fowler lived up to his name when he made off with the barrow and all of its apples, if you please; in 1871, bells pealed across the city when the unfortunate Sam 'The Fish' Salmon was washed away by a tidal wave of effluent when he was half-way down the sewage pipe; and in 1912, Tommy Thompson was disqualified when it was revealed he was really Reginald Smythe-Blenkinsop, the son of an aristocrat.

By the time of Smythe-Blenkinsop's deception, however, the Obstacle Race's run was almost at an end. In 1914 and 1915, thousands of urchins were sent to France to fight for king and country. Many paid the ultimate price; in 1916 at Verdun, the King's Own Barefoot Raggedly Rifle Brigade was decimated. By the end of the war the few urchins that remained were found proper work. They were also given shoes by a society who had grown squeamish about the sight of unshod feet. The competition was held sporadically throughout the 1920s and 1930s, but the abolition of the sovereign and the collapse of the British velvet industry were the final nails in its coffin. When London was blitzed in the Second World War, creating more fresh urchins than anyone dared to think about, the nation was too busy standing firm against Hitler to think about resurrecting an obstacle race. For a moment or two in 1941, Winston Churchill considered diverting resources to the manufacture of velvet and the importation of Cuban cigars, but in the end he decided it was best to concentrate on the war effort. History has shown he probably made the right choice.

TOMMY BREWER

Football

The winter of 1963 was a notoriously harsh one. Water was frozen and snow covered the ground from New Year's Day until April. For the footballers of second division Plymouth Argyle, faced with journeys of hundreds of miles up and down the country, the winter was even bleaker because they had Tommy Brewer to entertain them.

Tommy Brewer, Devon born and raised, had joined the club as a fifteen-year old apprentice in 1958. A strapping six-foot centre half, he'd combined his talent for football with a love of blues music. So deep was this passion that his wife Susan had bought him an acoustic guitar for Christmas. Three nights a week, training and matches permitting, he could be found in the pubs and clubs of Devon, picking away at the strings and wailing his heart out. Tragically for Tommy – and any pub regulars who happened to be in earshot – he was tone deaf with fingers like ripe bananas. So spectacularly awful was his singing and playing that he very rarely played a second gig at the same venue. Pubs had been known to go suddenly dark and bolt their doors when Tommy Brewer came ambling down the road, guitar slung over his shoulder, hoping to play a gig.

Tommy's team-mates were largely unaware of his passion until that bitter winter. Argyle had made a good start to the season and by early January 1963 the team were well placed in the second division for a promotion push. Unbeaten since late October and with a favourable run of fixtures to come, there was talk that Plymouth might finally reach the summit of English football for the first time in its history. It was then that a minor incident happened which was to have major repercussions for the future of Plymouth Argyle. Whilst parking the team bus prior to a trip to Rotherham, the driver lost control on a patch of ice and bumped into a gatepost, damaging the front bumper and the radio. The other Plymouth players clambered aboard, joking about the bent bumper and wondering whether the bus would manage the long trip to South Yorkshire. Tommy Brewer only noticed the broken radio. He rushed back to his house, picked up his guitar, and proceeded to play his own blues compositions to his team-mates for the eight-hour trip.

His songs had such titles as 'Slit My Throat Blues', 'Never Ending Ice Age' and an untitled number which opened with the line: 'Woke up this morning with a feeling we'd get thrashed at Rotherham'. By the time the coach reached the ground, the players were so emotionally drained that they succumbed to a walloping 6–0 defeat. Only Tommy showed any sort of form. He played more songs on the journey back to Devon – which took a lot longer due to worsening weather conditions – although not all of the players heard them. Three members of the team hired a taxi from their own pocket, and four others took the train.

The coach trip to Rotherham set the tone for the rest of Plymouth's season. They played eight further games away from home, and lost all of them. During these journeys Tommy's Argyle team-mates learned that his daughter had been ill. In 'Chickenpox Blues' he sang about: 'Those itchy skin rash, blisterin' pustule, cover me with calamine lotion blues'. 'Cheating Susan Blues' informed them that his wife had left him. Worst of all was a tortuous ten-hour journey to Middlesbrough in which the Argyle players were spared no detail of his dog's untimely death: 'I had me a wire-haired fox terrier – loved that doggie so; He got hit by a speedin' milkfloat – Lord, that ain't no way to go . . .' The dozen or so verses were accompanied by a noise that was meant to sound like a dying dog, and which was as tuneless as his playing.

By the end of the 1962–3 season Plymouth's promotion charge had petered out, and the team ended up in mid-table. The second the campaign ended Tommy Brewer was transferred to Torquay.

A fourth division team, the Gulls, as Torquay are known, enjoyed a decent start to the 1963–4 season and, after an unfortunate accident which destroyed Tommy's guitar, looked odds-on for promotion. Then, just before a tricky trip up north to Doncaster, he turned up with an electric guitar – claiming to be inspired by Bob Dylan no less – and a portable amplifier. Tommy entertained the team with his rendition of 'Got Me A Bad Feelin' About Playing Doncaster Rovers Blues' – a sentiment which turned out to be accurate. The promotion push was derailed, and Tommy Brewer was offloaded to fierce local rivals Exeter City.

Three years later, after a succession of short spells at Bristol City, Swindon Town, Bristol Rovers and Bourne-mouth, Tommy Brewer had run out of football clubs. He'd also run out of pubs where he could play his distinctive brand of music. By the summer of 1967 he'd joined non-league Gloucester City, but it only took one journey – an otherwise straightforward trip to Kidderminster – for his club colleagues to decide what to do. Scarcely a mile out of town on the way back home, while Tommy screeched passionately about the team's abject defeat, the coach suddenly pulled into a lay-by. The Gloucester players all pounced on him and, before he could react, Tommy and his guitar were dumped unceremoniously by the side of the road. Feeling sorry for himself, he was just about to compose a blues dirge to express how he felt about the situation when he heard the sound of music and laughter coming from a nearby field. On closer investigation it turned out to be the Kidderminster Folk Festival.

Several hours later, after he'd drunk eight pints of cider, eaten some cake of dubious provenance and made the acquaintance of a pretty girl called Saffron, Tommy Brewer was a changed man. When he composed his next song – at Saffron's house – the lyrics were about pixies and wizards, magical kingdoms and love.

A few months later, Tommy Brewer was turning out for his new team, Kidderminster Harriers. While it would be nice to report that those long journeys to away fixtures were lightened by the new uplifting songs that Tommy had written, it wouldn't be altogether true. His new compositions did extol the virtues of Kidderminster cattle market, his dog Sandy, the favourable interest rates he'd got for his mortgage and, of course, the baby that his new wife Saffron was expecting. But Tommy's playing – and his singing – was just as awful as it always had been. In any case, he was forbidden from playing his guitar on the Kidderminster team bus. The club already had a resident musician – goalkeeper Alan 'Squeeze Box' Spencer, whose depressing accordion-accompanied sea shanties made every journey seem ten times as long.

REUBEN SMITH, AKA 'THE PROFESSOR'

Wrestling

'Greetings grapple fans' were the familiar words with which commentator Kent Walton would introduce the wrestling every Saturday afternoon on ITV throughout the 1960s and 1970s. There were no shortage of grapplers, but to really stand out from the crowd and become a household name a wrestler needed a good gimmick. Big Daddy had the unique distinction of being fat – as did Giant Haystacks – while the wrestler known to the world as Kendo Nagasaki wore a Japanese samurai warrior mask to create an aura of fear and mystery, something that mere trunks couldn't possibly provide.

A wrestler equally as good, if not quite as infamous, was Reuben Smith, aka 'The Professor'. While his opponents would strip off their dressing gowns and prowl around the ring snarling, Smith would approach it dressed in mortar board and cape, with a pair of half-moon spectacles perched on his nose. To the uninitiated it looked as if comedy actor Will Hay had stepped out of one of his films. This charade continued as 'The Professor', still

bumbling along, head buried in a book, climbed up the steps to the ring, fell through the ropes and landed on the canvas. Then, picking himself up and facing the aggressive snarl of the wrestler opposite, he would tear off his costume, under which he would be dressed in regulation boots and trunks. At the end of each round, while his opponents gargled water and spat, 'The Professor' would slip on his spectacles and scribble away on a blackboard, seemingly oblivious to what was happening around him. It didn't matter though – 'The Professor' usually won in the end.

But if the paying public thought Reuben Smith's behaviour was nothing more than a display of showmanship, they couldn't have been more wrong. For Reuben Smith – while not technically a professor – was one of Britain's most gifted intellectuals. Away from the wrestling mat, Reuben Smith was an unofficial member of the Brains Trust, as well as a lecturer in thermodynamics at the Goldberg Institute in central London. His papers on any number of subjects – from arts to sciences – were always eagerly anticipated. The blackboard scribbles, far from a prop, were critically important – whether they were Latin translations, calculus or some scientific theory.

Reuben Smith was born in Gospel Oak in north London in 1948. He first showed he could look after himself as a youngster in the school playground, when he caught 'Basher' Higgins in a headlock and forced the class bully to yell for his mummy. After that nobody ever dared to try and steal one of Reuben's gobstoppers. He rejected the offered post of school bully and elected instead to concentrate on his studies. This farsightedness reaped dividends. Six years later he'd won a scholarship to Merton College, Oxford, where he studied Philosophy, Physics and Medieval Poetry – and took up wrestling.

The Merton College Grappler's Society didn't have a proper club headquarters, so matches took place on the main quadrangle. A set of ropes and posts would be erected after matins and each afternoon the college wrestlers would grunt and groan on the springy turf. Crowds of baying undergraduates would cheer from their dormitory windows. In no time at all, Reuben Smith became Merton College champion, a title he won by defeating Thomas 'Frenchy' Fielding, a second-year Modern Languages student. Once the wrestling had resumed after the winter break, Reuben pinned Joseph Montague, aka 'The Brasenose Bruiser', on College Green, winning the Oxford University Belt. The following year, after beating Cambridge University's masked wrestling champion, 'The Cam Tiger', Reuben Smith was awarded a full blue. As well as a splendid looking tie and jacket, this entitled him to wear a special dressing gown made of shot silk, with the college crest on the pocket. On the reverse, Smith included his own flourish – a silhouette of a head wearing a mortar board. When he next took to the wrestling ring, his fellow students began cheering for 'The Professor' and the nickname stuck.

Reuben Smith graduated with first-class honours in 1969, but found work as a philosopher and medieval poetry expert hard to come by. He offered to wrestle all-comers for the vacant position of narrator on a forthcoming radio series on *The Canterbury Tales*, but the Director General of the BBC dismissed the idea as nonsense. So, to bring in an income while he looked for work, Reuben Smith turned to the world of professional wrestling. It was a popular sport in the late 1960s and weekly bouts were held in town halls throughout the country. Smith found himself an agent, Jake Stupples, who recommended that his client adopt a personality for the ring. Stupples already looked after 'Leopard Man' Mkunzi, Apache Atkinson, 'Saintly' Stephen Jones and Ken O'Keefe, the self-styled 'Sheikh of Pontefract'. Reuben dusted off his cape, had a customized headmaster's outfit made, bought a flashy new pair of boots and was all set to go as a wrestler.

Reuben Smith got his big break in March 1971 when he faced Peter 'Praise the Lord' Bartholomew, a wrestler who wore a dog collar, in a televised bout. Ten million viewers saw 'The Professor' get scandalously beaten, when Bartholomew produced a metal-studded Bible from his corner and knocked Smith out. A few old women in the front row expressed their outrage, but the result stood. 'The Professor' appeared on TV on a dozen further occasions – all the time mixing his wrestling with philosophy, astrophysics, applied mathematics, woodwork, French and jazz tap.

During this time, Reuben Smith had found work as a freelance 'Ideas Man' with Imperial College, a post which left him with plenty of free time to wrestle. His great intellect was acknowledged by frequent appearances on the *Brains Trust* programme – in which some of the country's leading intellectuals debated the issues of the day – and on *Boffin Island*, a comedy show about science.

The economy took a sharp downturn in 1973, and British professional wrestling was not immune from the harsher financial climate. Many big names quit the sport – seasoned grapplers like Johnny Handsome, Max 'The Shark' Sharkey and Alan 'No Gimmick' Rutherford. With venues closing, and TV wrestling under threat, grapplers took whatever work they could. So, on a rainy night in May 1974, Reuben Smith appeared on the bill at Rochdale's run-down Queen Alexandra Hall, while also working – it is believed – on a formula for cold fusion. Alas, we will never know. In his bout against Clarence 'The Caveman' Kaufman – a prehistoric themed wrestler who was also a lecturer in Physical Geography – a time-honoured trick went badly wrong. During a spot of play acting, 'The Caveman' began savagely beating 'The Professor' with a club he kept propped up in his corner. It was part of his stage act, and no one in the audience batted an eyelid – not even when 'The Professor' was carried from the ring to his dressing room. Only then, when Reuben failed to leap to his feet, did people suspect that something was amiss. To his horror Jake Stupples discovered that the foam rubber club which 'The Caveman' normally took on stage was still in Kaufman's locker. The solid wooden club, the one he showed to sceptics who assumed all the fights were rigged, had mistakenly been taken on stage instead and used to batter 'The Professor' on the skull.

Reuben Smith, alas, had sustained serious head injuries and, despite being rushed to Rochdale General Hospital, nothing could be done. He remained there in a persistent vegetative state – fed, ironically, through a capillary tube device of his own design – until in 1983 the machine was switched off by Terry 'The Terminator' Bradshaw in a ceremonial unplugging ceremony.

'Professor' Reuben Smith left many legacies, but his solution to the knotty problem of cold fusion was not one of them. His precious blackboard, which apparently contained the formula all written out, had been wiped clean by drops of rain coming through the leaky ceiling. A number of scientists – one or two of whom were wrestlers – tried to interpret the smudges, but it was all to no avail. The blackboard was last seen in October 1977, when 'Little John' Sherwood smashed it to pieces over the head of Dave Butterworth, aka 'The Sheriff of Nottingham', happily with no ill effects. It might not have been what 'The Professor' wanted, but it made for a good show.

STEVENSON USK

Naked Fishing

There is surely nobody in this country that has done more to further the cause of naked fishing than Stevenson Usk. The rector of All Souls Craggfoot, in Cumbria, Reverend Usk is well known to readers of *Fishermen's World* magazine thanks to photos of him and his handily placed carp or chub.

As much as he loves fishing in the raw, the so-called 'Knickerless Parson' spares his parishioners their blushes. (In any case, preaching in the nude is illegal north of the River Trent.) A man of the cloth in the pulpit, he only becomes a man of no cloth at the end of the service, when he strips off his surplice and heads for Coniston Water or Bassenthwaite to indulge both his passions at once.

Stevenson Usk was born near Barrow-in-Furness in 1950. As he explained in his autobiography, *No Flies On Me*, he gained a love of nudity from his parents, Arthur and Elspeth, who ran a hillside farm and could often be seen herding sheep or planting barley in the altogether. As well as being unashamed of their bodies, the couple were also convinced it did wonders for toughening the skin. It was a controversial belief, and one that had very likely cost the lives of

Stevenson's elder siblings, both of whom died of exposure – although he somehow survived. Arthur Usk was also a deeply religious man, and finding no conflict between his love of the Bible and naturism, could often be seen preaching in the Lakeland villages, with nothing to hide behind but scripture. An unorthodox firebrand, he made for an impressive sight – even on the coldest of days.

Young Stevenson inherited this passion, and when he was old enough enrolled at St Colin's College of Divinity in Hexham. St Colin's had a liberal reputation, and nudity played a big part in the curriculum. Undergraduates were encouraged to leave not just their prejudices but their clothes at the front door. Stevenson joined the college's Nude Angling Club and could regularly be seen on the banks of the North Tyne, hoping to catch something. The members of the Nude Angling Club were often subjected to taunts and ridicules from an ill-informed public, but had learned to turn the other cheek. Sarcastic remarks such as 'That's a tiddler you've got there mate', 'I don't think much of your tackle' or 'You need to hold your rod a bit tighter' were always met with a smile. Not that there wasn't the occasional mishap on the riverbank. Nettles and thorns were always a problem, and a careless bit of casting could often mean an end to the day's fishing.

When he graduated in 1973, the Reverend Usk began looking for a parish in his native Lakeland which had nudist sympathies, not to mention decent fishing waters nearby. He soon found one. The vicar of All Souls Craggfoot had recently been defrocked (only figuratively) and Stevenson Usk was given the chance to step into the breach.

Britain is known for its prudish attitude to public displays of nudity, so it came as no surprise to Usk when some members of his congregation took objection to his angling in the buff. A torchlit procession marched to the rectory, where they began chanting 'No flashing when fishing' and 'Boot out the angler with the dangler'. To begin with Reverend Usk tried to reason with them – quoting passages from the Bible which extolled the virtues of naked flesh – and when that didn't work he mooned at them from his bedroom window.

In August 1976 Stevenson Usk qualified for the finals of the British Nude Coarse Fishing Championships – or as their detractors preferred to call them, the Extremely Coarse Fishing Championships. The event was held on the River Tay in Scotland, where the long summer drought meant water levels were exceptionally low, and many nude angling fans thought there would be nothing to see. But using all the skill he'd mustered as a naked fisherman, the Reverend Usk landed a whopper. The forty-pound pike he reeled in brought cheers from the crowds and remains to this day the heaviest fish ever caught in Britain by a man wearing no clothes.

Usk's success gained him selection for the British Angling Team for the World Nude Games, which were scheduled for Norway in 1977. It proved to be a double triumph for Stevenson Usk, not only helping Britain to unexpectedly beat Canada, the world's foremost nude fishing nation, but also claiming the individual gold. It was the start of a glittering career.

In 1980 Reverend Usk met Sarah, a nude kite-flying champion whose string had got tangled in some trees right next to where he was fishing. It was love at first sight. The pair married the following year and had four children. Since then Stevenson Usk has proved adept at juggling his balls – fulfilling his duties as a rector while keeping his family happy and staying at the top in the world of nudist angling.

There are many who believe that Stevenson Usk's sporting achievements deserve greater recognition. After all, he's dominated his sport: seven times world champion, nine times European champion – and in 1990 became the first ever winner of the 'Starkers Slam' when he won all four major naked fishing titles in the same calendar year. Some say it's only the Reverend Usk's unconventional lifestyle that has prevented him being honoured by the Queen. Perhaps there are concerns about a naked man being photographed in Buckingham Palace. But there's also the tricky question about where Her Majesty would pin the medal.

KENNETH TOPLEY-ADAMS AND THE HON. EDGAR MUYNINGS

Carriage Driving

One of the world's most elegant sports is surely carriage driving, where at its best man, horse and wooden box work together in perfect harmony. So it may come as a surprise to discover that this most genteel of recreations spawned one of sport's bitterest rivalries. Forget Manchester United and Liverpool, Celtic and Rangers or Manchester United and Leeds – Kenneth Topley-Adams and the Hon. Edgar Muynings outdid all of them.

Topley-Adams and Muynings were both born in 1961 and raised in the village of Great Arden, in Buckinghamshire. The two boys were best friends at nursery school and enjoyed an idyllic childhood, with more fresh air, holidays, treats, money and indulgence than was probably good for them. They could often be seen racing their bikes down country lanes, pulling custom-made handcarts behind them, invoking jealousy in any other child who saw them, and holding up traffic for miles. But better even than bicycles, both boys loved horses. Young Edgar, the scion of minor counties gentry, persuaded his parents to buy him a pony. Kenneth came from more common stock, but what they lacked in breeding his parents made up for with money. With no desire to see their child outdone, they splashed out on a slightly bigger pony than Edgar's. It wasn't one for the jumps, so a cart was constructed for it to pull around the local fields, while Kenneth stood on the back, shouting his head off. No sooner had he seen Kenneth's cart, than Edgar retrained his pony to pull a bigger cart.

Neither boy acknowledged the other's ponies, which were exchanged for horses as they became teenagers. The moments they spent in one another's company enacting their horse-based fantasies soon became nothing but memories.

It was while watching the 1974 Horse of the Year Show that both boys experienced a revelatory moment. In addition to the usual fare of show-jumping and pony derbies there had been a display of carriage driving by the Duke of Edinburgh. An acknowledged expert at the sport, he'd managed to win his race after his opponent's carriage mysteriously sustained a broken axle. The next day both boys ordered their fathers to build them the grandest carriage that Buckinghamshire had ever seen. Having no idea what the previous best was, both men set about their task with relish. Things were certainly easier for Mr Topley-Adams, whose wealth stemmed from his ownership of the Topley-Adams Timber Company, Buckinghamshire's biggest wood dealership. He knocked up a three-storey high faux Elizabethan manor house on wheels for his son, which sadly proved too much for the horse, which managed two paces before dropping down dead from a heart attack.

As they became young men, Edgar and Kenneth grew

further apart on account of a woman – which so often happens. They had both fallen for the charms of Clorinda Usher, the daughter of one of the county's tallest land-owners, and each night would parade up and down outside her gated mansion in their increasingly elaborate carriages, decorated with paintings and sprayed with pheromones. In the end, Clorinda chose Edgar or, as he was known by then, the Honourable Edgar. Thwarted in love, Kenneth har-boured a burning resentment, but waited till the couple's wedding day before he acted upon it. As Clorinda arrived at the church – curiously, not in a carriage – Kenneth sped past at full gallop, splashing her wedding dress with mud and detritus.

For several years the two men avoided one another – winning rival carriage-driving tournaments almost at will – until they finally clashed at the All England Carriage Driving Championships in 1986. Kenneth Topley-Adams won a tight contest by the narrowest of margins, but the Hon. Edgar objected to Topley-Adams's box. He accused the winner of cheating by driving a deliberately light box made of bamboo that had been painted to look like wood. In turn Topley-Adams accused Muynings of waxing his carriage wheels to make them run faster. The argument descended into a fist fight in which both men sustained black eyes and flattened top hats.

Each time the two carriage drivers met after that the incidents escalated. In 1987, at the Lowestoft Show, Muynings's carriage caught fire when it careered into a burning oil drum that had inexplicably been put there at the last minute. Later that year Topley-Adams discovered his carriage had been doused with paraffin – somewhat dangerous when he was attempting to navigate the 'River of

Fire' at the Merioneth Carriage Driving Festival. Then, at the Equine Show at Olympia, following an anonymous tip off that it was concealing IRA explosives, Muynings's carriage was dismantled and detonated by an army bomb disposal squad, while his horses were subjected to an intimate cavity search in full view of the Queen.

In 1991, at the request of show-jumping legend Raymond Brooks-Ward, the two drivers agreed to take part in a novelty race for Comic Relief. The theme for the competition was carriages from well-known songs. Kenneth Topley-Adams chose a magnificent Surrey with a fringe on top, while Edgar Muynings added some wheels to a sledge and created a one-horse open sleigh. As it turned out, both of the rivals' vehicles struggled with the boggy Newmarket conditions. The race was won by an amateur carriage enthusiast, Ernie Cooke, who proved he did have the fastest milk cart in the west.

Unable to reconcile their differences, both Topley-Adams and Muynings swore that they would not rest until the other was dead – a vicious outburst which ruined an otherwise harmless episode of *Country File*. What neither man realized was that it would come to pass at the now infamous Cross Berkshire Carriage Cavalcade of 1994. This gruelling race required the drivers to steer their horses and carriages over all manner of terrains – along streets, through fields, streams, uphill, down-dale and across twenty-five miles of open countryside from Slough in the east to the finish line at Hungerford. More than a hundred entrants – each driving a four-horse carriage – lined up outside the Tesco Superstore near Slough railway station. It was a scene of utter pandemonium. But once the race had got under way, it only took a couple of miles before Topley-Adams and

Muynings had shown their class and left the others far behind.

The first incident happened as they hurtled across Farnham Common. While Muynings whipped his horses into a frenzied gallop, a set of razor-sharp knives shot out from the hubcap of his carriage wheels. He manoeuvred over to Topley-Adams, but the blades snapped off before they could do any damage. A few miles later when they crossed the Berkshire Downs, a posse of men on horseback swooped out of the hills whooping and hollering and began firing arrows at Edgar Muynings. They were friends of Topley-Adams, all local members of the Geronimo Appreciation Society and dressed for the part. Muynings took an arrow in the shoulder, but ignoring the pain produced a Winchester rifle from under his seat with which he despatched two of the Red Indians. After the rest had scattered he turned his rifle on his bitter enemy. Topley-Adams pulled out a Colt .45 and began firing back.

By Newbury both men had run out of bullets, and the two carriages came crashing together, sparks flying as metal rubbed against metal. As the horses' hooves thundered towards Hungerford, first Topley-Adams then Muynings tried to grab the other's harness before swinging desperate punches at one another. So wrapped up in their struggle were they that neither saw the 'Dangerous Bridge Ahead' sign, and both sets of horses, carriages and men plunged over the edge on to the M4 motorway below. The two men were killed instantly as were, unfortunately, eighteen other people – innocent victims who ploughed into the mangled wreckage of wood, metal and horse flesh.

Edgar's widow fervently hoped that her husband's funeral would see a gathering of the great and the good of the equine world, but Clorinda's hopes were cruelly dashed. She discovered that Edgar had been a recent convert to Zoroastrianism, and instead of a lavish burial his body was left on top of a stone pillar, where his bones were picked clean by crows. Kenneth Topley-Adams's will decreed that his body be buried inside his grandest carriage. It took them four days to dig his grave.

MAURICE DIGNAM

Underwater Hoop Plunge

There's a simple reason why no one recalls the greatest sporting achievement of Maurice Dignam. He might have been in the right place, but it was not the right time, for at the moment of his unlikely triumph, nobody was watching.

Born in Coventry in 1933, Maurice Dignam survived the Blitz and by the tender age of twenty-five had become Deputy Assistant Head of the city's central library. An expert handler of scissors, paste and black ink, he was given editorial responsibility for newspapers and books. This mainly involved cutting out the horse-racing results and betting tips, or any article which expressed anything derogatory about Coventry, before the papers were handed over to the general public. Maurice was also the keeper of the key to the special cupboard which held the solitary, unexpurgated copy of *Lady Chatterley's Lover* – at that time considered the naughtiest book in Britain, if not the world. He made good use of this privileged position, borrowing the book most weekends, and knew more rude words than anyone else in Coventry.

But four-letter expletives were not the only thing that

FORGOTTEN SPORTING HEROES No. 40

MAURICE DIGNAM
UNDERWATER HOOP PLUNGE

Maurice had learned from the book. He'd also fathered eight children – five of them with his wife, Nellie – most of which were conceived in his potting shed on the allotment. These amorous trysts had not been without their consequences – on one occasion a lady friend had got her foot stuck in a watering can, while on another, two trays of runner bean seedlings were carelessly destroyed during the passionate throes of lovemaking.

It was his editorial duties which first alerted Maurice to the Olympic Games. A small article in the *Coventry Telegraph* included a picture of a rare Japanese silk print which depicted pearl divers swimming through hoops on the seabed. The underwater hoop plunge, the piece concluded, would be one of the fringe cultural events at the forthcoming Tokyo Olympics.

A keen member of the Coventry sub-aquatic club – when he wasn't reading *Lady Chatterley* or spending time in his potting shed – Maurice immediately declared his intention to compete in the event at the Games. When the evening's session finished at his local pool, he was given permission to practise on his own. So, while the attendant spent a couple of hours reading *Lady Chatterley's Lover* by torchlight, Maurice plunged through hoops he'd weighted to the bottom of the pool. For two months he did this, subsisting on a diet or crisps, Bounty bars and scalding hot chicken soup from the vending machine.

By the summer of 1964 Maurice Dignam was ready. He packed his trunks, said goodbye to Nellie and the library, and headed out to Tokyo. It was an expensive journey, but Maurice managed to pay for it out of his own pocket. He raised the money by a judicious use of the betting tips he'd cut out of the newspapers, by loaning out *Lady Chatterley's*

Lover and by selling a bumper crop of runner beans that hadn't been squashed during illicit sexual encounters.

But instead of a generous greeting from the Japanese hosts, Maurice was surprised to find himself shunned at the airport, despite wearing the official British team blazer and slacks. He soon found out why. The Japanese people had put all their hopes into winning the underwater hoop plunge, and had not issued an invitation to any foreign entrants. It turned out that Maurice Dignam had been privy to the only news report on the underwater hoop plunge that had managed to reach the outside world. This leak had brought such shame on the organizer of the event that he had been required to fall on his sword – and when he proved unwilling to do so he was pushed on to the sharpened point of someone else's.

The Japanese hoop plungers, convinced they would have the run of the competition to themselves, had not really bothered to train for the event and proved no match for the librarian from Coventry. However many hoops a rival plunged through, Maurice Dignam would manage more. All those months of training, and all those cups of scalding hot chicken soup, had paid off.

The Japanese paying public, not best pleased at seeing a foreigner beating them at their own game, left their seats in droves. By the time Maurice took his final plunge the gold medal was already his – but there was nobody watching. Unfortunately, there was nobody watching back home in the UK, either. Everyone had tuned in to watch *Coronation Street* on ITV rather than the Olympics on the BBC. A fire had broken out in the Rover's Return, killing tragic Meg Foster, the pretty young barmaid who was due to get married the following week. The British press contingent, who had requested the episode be relayed to Japan by satellite, missed Maurice's performance as well.

The underwater hoop plunge was subsequently hushed up by the Japanese authorities when the truth about it finally emerged. A sharp-eyed archivist in the Tokyo Silk Print Museum noticed that what had been assumed to be underwater hoops were no such thing. They were, instead, rings caused by a coffee cup that a previous slapdash curator had put there.

After his surprising, if low key triumph, Maurice Dignam decided to remain in Japan. He moved to the outskirts of Tokyo and wrote a children's book called *Leroy's Yellow Lorry*, which became a surprise bestseller in spite of being very difficult for Japanese people to pronounce. In 1965 he settled down with a girl called Masako and had four children – two of them with Masako.

JULIUS FRUMNEY

Honest Running

Julius Frumney, the progenitor of the sport he christened Honest Running, was one of the great zealots of Victorian Britain. Not that Frumney would have described himself in those terms. He would have considered himself instead a paragon of Honest Common Sense.

It was in 1881 when Julius Frumney first came to public attention. In March of that year he was apprehended in the South Kensington Museum while hacking the marble penis off a Michelangelo sculpture with a hammer and chisel. Far from being castigated for this piece of artistic vandalism, the 25-year-old Frumney found himself lauded by the museum's moral guardians. In due course he was given carte blanche to dismember every other statue in the collection and, once his chisel had been re-sharpened, Frumney did exactly that.

His actions, indeed, started the craze which came to be known in Britain as 'Penis Frenzy'. In museums and art galleries across the country eager young men took up their tools and followed Frumney's example. Local newspapers carried advertisements exhorting men to gather for a spot of 'chap chopping' or what they mischievously referred to in the music halls as 'going off half-cocked'. The penises on Britain's classical sculptures disappeared almost overnight. Nobody, however, carried out these acts with quite as much fervour as Julius Frumney. At the Piccadilly Museum in Manchester, he set an all-comers' record when he knocked off six marble willies in three-quarters of an hour. He dashed from gallery to gallery on his self-appointed mission without once breaking sweat in a display of what he referred to as 'Honest Running'.

It should be pointed out that after he removed the offending appendages, Frumney would fill the gap with a marble fig leaf – specially manufactured in his own workshop. The fig leaves came in three distinct sizes – small, medium and maiden aunt's swoon. Frumney made a small fortune from the enterprise, which he hoped to export to continental Europe. Unfortunately for him, an offer to 'de-chap' Michelangelo's *David* was rejected by the Italian authorities, who said that the Pope would disapprove.

Frumney made rather less money from his attempts to cover naked female statuary with sacks. The overabundance of hessian in late Victorian England meant it was always unlikely to be a great money-spinner. Nevertheless he continued to pursue his ideals – his chief success coming in early 1882 when he travelled to Paris and threw a coal sack over the Venus de Milo, a feat made easier by her lack of arms.

In 1884 Julius Frumney's attention was grabbed by a sporting innovation which drew him away from lewd marble statues. For the first time the Wimbledon lawn tennis championships had thrown open their doors to women competitors, so Frumney, armed with handfuls of sacks, ran honestly to south-west London. To his chagrin the club gatekeeper refused to admit him to the grounds, so Frumney was obliged to watch proceedings through a hole in the hedge along with two dozen admirers of the bare female ankle. The following day he returned, this time with copies of his pamphlet: 'Against the Monstrous Regiment of Bare-Fleshed Strumpets and Harlots'. Frumney handed out copies to passers-by and when they refused to take any more he shoved the remainder through the hole in the hedge.

Julius Frumney's single-minded activities had not gone unnoticed by the men who were shaping the sporting future of Great Britain. His prodigious athletic feats – running across London delivering leaflets and defacing statues, not to mention his forthright views on women – inevitably brought him to the attention of the London Corinthian Athletic Club. The Corinthians were a like-minded group, whose founder, Captain Evans, had angered the National Gallery when he'd daubed some britches on a Botticelli nude without permission. Evans offered Julius Frumney immediate life membership. Frumney was flattered by this suggestion, but rejected it when he saw the club's running outfits, which consisted of a long-sleeved singlet and shorts. The singlet was just about permissible, but Frumney took issue with the notion of wearing any form of trouser which stopped short of the shoe. No matter that the shorts resembled pantaloons and finished a goodly length below the knee – they left part of the leg flesh exposed. A compromise suggestion of long club socks was loftily dismissed. Furthermore, Frumney disapproved of the Corinthians' energetic and unrestrained athletic style, which he insisted went counter to the philosophy of his own Honest Running. An Honest Runner, contended Frumney, went about his business fully clothed and without perspiring. Sweating was the province of continentals, such as the onion-eating French or the oil-obsessed Mediterranean nations. No English gentleman worth his salt could possibly deign to compete on such terms. If sweating were permissible in athletic events, then in no time at all European athletes would be snapping at the heels of their British betters. It would be Honest Running, as far as he was concerned, or no running at all.

In 1886, amidst great pomp and ceremony – two particularly British specialities – Julius Frumney launched his own Honest Running Club for Englishmen. As an incentive, he offered a free chisel to every new member he accepted. Frumney's standards proved so exacting, however, that in the event he was only required to hand over eight chisels. Most applicants were rejected for perspiring, for not having a fulsome enough beard or for coming from too far north. Frumney refused to believe that anybody who lived more than an Honest Walk from London could possibly call himself a gentleman – another unbending requirement. In the scorching August heat of that year the first, and indeed only, British Honest Running Championships were held in St Albans. As well as competing, Julius Frumney appointed himself race referee, and over the course of the two-mile event promptly disqualified every one of the other eight athletes. All of them had either broken sweat or were on the verge of doing so.

In many ways, it proved to be Julius Frumney's last sporting hurrah. Throughout the 1880s evidence emerged that fresh air was beneficial to the limbs, and the belief gained ground that a gentleman who exposed his legs had no reason to feel ashamed. In addition, a little honest sweat was also considered beneficial – provided, of course, it wasn't a lady's. Faced with this overwhelming scientific evidence, the fashion for Honest Sport simply melted away. Footballers, rugby players and athletes all began to expose their flesh. The only sport which resisted this new trend was cricket, which rejected the idea of shorts after the dismally cold summer of 1887.

Following the debacle of the British Honest Running Championships, Julius Frumney more or less disappeared from the world of competitive sport. He made the national news again in 1888 when he was questioned in connection with the brutal Whitechapel killings, but he was soon discounted as a potential 'Jack the Ripper'. He had, after all, spent the year in the West Country making drapes to fit around table legs to cover their wooden nakedness. It was while he was taking the measurements of an especially immodest table leg in Devizes that he met the twenty-year-old Miss Tews, an especially prim piano teacher. After an Honest Courtship, the pair were married and subsequently had thirteen children, all of them no doubt conceived during Honest Sex in a totally darkened bedroom.

Julius Frumney tragically lost his life in 1904. While on an Honest Saunter along the country lanes near his Somerset home, he was struck by a new fangled Lanchester motor car and killed instantly. He was buried, fully clothed, in what he would doubtless have called an Honest Funeral. All six pall-bearers sported magnificent beards, and not one of them broke sweat as they carried his coffin.

COLONEL J.H. MANDERS

Disabled Elephant Polo

Colonel John Henry 'J.H.' Manders liked to portray himself as one of the Indian continent's great philanthropists. He had, after all, opened the first field hospital for wounded elephants in Hyderabad. Keen to offer sanctuary to these magnificent beasts, a stream of disfigured pachyderms was welcomed by the colonel with open arms. But what appears on the surface to be an example of kind-hearted animal welfare was in fact nothing of the sort. For the unfortunate elephants – missing the odd foot, tusks, ears, tails and, tragically, the occasional trunk, had all been mutilated by Colonel Manders himself.

The India of the early 1920s offered great business opportunities to the entrepreneurially minded. Tea and spices were hugely profitable ventures, and following the Great Exhibition of 1923 there was a sudden craze for umbrella stands fashioned from elephants' feet. Demand soon outstripped supply and the price of these novelty items – which were fully waterproofed and difficult to tip over – went through the roof. The colonel, with an eye for an easy profit and a ready supply of fit and healthy elephants on his doorstep, immediately went to work. He contacted his friend, Mr N. Prajwal Gupta, the master baker of Hyderabad, and ordered several thousand sticky buns – the elephant's well-documented weakness – to sprinkle as bait. Unable to resist, the animals lumbered towards Manders's specially built compound, where they were quickly separated from one of their feet. After the innards were scooped out and made slightly less gruesome with a coat of tar, the highly desirable umbrella stands were shipped off to England – along with a selection of fly swats (tails) and grey-coloured jaunty hats (ears). A small number of trunks were also sent to Australia to supplement the market for didgeridoos. Within a few short years Colonel Manders had established a string of elephant 'hospitals' the length and breadth of India, and had made the market for elephant by-products his own.

Manders did not regard himself as an unreasonably cruel man, and his intention was always that once the animal had recovered from its ordeal it would be released back into the wild, where it could serve its original purpose – as sport for hunters. A noble enough plan, it backfired because the colonel had failed to anticipate that the three-legged animals would prove no match for a well-aimed rifle. To make things worse, the hunters complained that an elephant deprived of its ears, tusks or trunk made for a most unsatisfactory mounted head on a living-room wall. So, rather than let the poor animals hobble aimlessly around India, Manders devised another plan, for which he has passed into sporting legend.

In June 1928 the colonel announced that he was forming the British Empire's first ever disabled elephant polo league. There would be two divisions each comprising twelve teams and matches would be decided, somewhat appropriately, over three legs. Disappointingly for Colonel Manders, his own team, the Hyderabad Hopalongs, were pipped for the title in 1928 by the Nagpur No-Tuskers.

The league, alas, did not survive for long. Manders's scheme to make a fortune from elephants was undone by a rival colonel – the more enterprising and far less scrupulous George Derek 'G.D.' Piddock. The so-called 'Butcher of Bahawalpur' had no thought for either the animals' well being or the umbrella-stand market back home, and he began slaughtering elephants indiscriminately. Rather than just a single foot and a disabled elephant, Piddock instead had four feet and a dead one. Soon Great Britain was awash with elephant's foot umbrella stands and wrinkly grey soft tops for motor cars with their unmistakable tail dangling over the rear window. With the price at rock bottom, it no longer made economic sense to butcher elephants or even slice one of their legs off. Facing financial ruin, in August 1931 Colonel Manders organized one last disabled elephant polo match between the Hyderabad Hopalongs and the Orissa One-Ears. Knowing full well it would be the final game the colonel ordered extra sticky buns as a treat from Mr Gupta. It was to prove a fatal mistake. The elephants – those with trunks at any rate – smelled the buns from some distance away and, driven wild with desire, ran, hopped or trundled over to the Indian baker. Colonel Manders, atop a frisky three-legger called Jinty with a particularly sweet tusk, was knocked to the ground and crushed to death in the stampede. As sticky ends go, it was an especially sticky one.

It would be poetic justice to suggest that the colonel's previous behaviour caught up with him, and that after his death his leg was hollowed out and used as a doorstop, or that his teeth were made into miniature chessmen. There is, however, no evidence that anything even remotely like that ever happened.

BROTHER REG

Darts

Few would dispute the fact that Brother Reg, born plain Reginald Duffery in Doncaster in 1952, is one of the finest Franciscan monks ever to have played the game of darts. Before Reg came on the scene, Brother Clement, the 'Double Top Dominican' and 'Bullseye Bertram', the 'Trappist with the Tungsten', were perceived to be the best darts-playing monks.

Reg Duffery began his sporting career as a promising junior footballer. He had trials with Doncaster Rovers and Bradford Park Avenue, but when he was rejected by his beloved Leeds United, young Reginald sought solace in religion. Within two weeks of being turned down by Don Revie, he had abandoned all his worldly goods and possessions – apart from a hooded brown robe and a pair of sandals – and become a member of the Order of St Francis.

His living quarters – on the outskirts of Ripon – were rudimentary. A rusting bedstead with an uncomfortably sprung mattress took up most of the space – the only decoration on the wall being a dartboard, superimposed with a portrait of Satan. The picture itself was largely

undamaged, although the wall around it was peppered with dart holes. The previous incumbent, Brother Honorius, had evidently been an appalling darts player, but Reg had a steady aim and each evening, by the light of a flickering candle, he would throw darts at the board. In no time at all, Satan's nostrils and eyeballs had been reduced to pulp – so accurate was Brother Reg's aim.

A visiting Carmelite monk, Brother 'Three Flights' Theosiphus (the former Bert Wilson) noted Reg's proficiency with the darts and recommended him for the Ripon and District Licensed Victuallers Darts League. Convinced that he could make plenty of converts, and divert some men to the path of righteousness while they enjoyed a pint and a game of darts, Brother Reg accepted.

It is said that the road to darts greatness is a tough and uncompromising one, and for Brother Reg it was particularly hard. For instead of catching the bus to the Dog and Trumpet or walking to the Bishop's Mitre, Reg insisted on expressing his devotion by crawling on all fours, in honour of his favourite saint, Gideon of Tyre. His first match, alas, was at the Victoria Arms, some fifteen miles away, and the game was long finished by the time he reached the saloon door. The sight of the crawling monk, his hands and knees bloodied and callused, caused consternation among the locals, especially when he refused any treatment for his injuries. The only thing Brother Reg would allow himself was a few drinks. Under Franciscan rules, a monk is free to consume alcoholic drink – but only if it has an appropriately religious name. So, after several pints of Abbot Ale and a few bags of 'Laughing Friar' brand pork scratchings (the same rule applies to bar snacks), Brother Reg crawled home.

He allowed plenty of time for his next match at the Dun

Cow, and despite having knees caked with blood and hands so gashed by sharp gravel he could barely grip his darts, Reg managed to win the match. A few glasses of Blue Nun dulled the pain, and then it was back once more to his humble little hermitage.

Brother Reg was crowned Ripon and District darts champion in 1974 and won the overall prize for the whole of North Yorkshire in 1975. His latter triumph was especially remarkable, bearing in mind that Reg had missed several matches in the summer. Forced to crawl alongside several miles of idling traffic caught up in Bank Holiday roadworks on the A61, he'd been overcome by fumes. It was only thanks to a kindly motorist, who revived Reg by dabbing Benedictine liqueur on his lips, that the Franciscan's life was saved. He spent the next few weeks recovering in his uncomfortable bed, throwing the occasional dart at Satan.

The sight of Brother Reg was a familiar one to motorists in North Yorkshire throughout the 1970s and 1980s, as he crawled his way to and from pubs. Improvements in road-building technology proved beneficial to the ground-bound monk, who found the softer, more knee-friendly tar helped his speed. Not that the Doncaster-born Franciscan was a believer in easy living. If he perceived a road to be too smooth – or if, during a rare moment of weakness, his thoughts turned to a comely looking barmaid – he'd crawl over some gravelly bits or head straight through the nearest patch of nettles. Should that fail to work, he'd jab himself in the thighs with his darts.

But it wasn't just the roads that were changing in 1980s Great Britain. As well as better tar, mobile phones and home computers were becoming commonplace, although conversely, roadside rubbish bins had become significantly rarer in an effort to foil the IRA and their bombs. Social attitudes were changing too, and while the Red Lion Hotel now welcomed same sex couples, in 1987 they turned away Brother Reg for contravening their 'No Monks' Habits or Sandals in the Saloon' rule. Many pubs were given facelifts, too, replacing their old dartboards with quiz machines and video jukeboxes.

By 1988, age and many miles of road were starting to catch up with North Yorkshire's most famous darts-throwing Franciscan. On an autumn evening in October of that year – possibly after too much mead – he mistakenly crawled through some dog mess at the side of the B6265. As usual Brother Reg refused to do anything about it and, by the time of his next game at the Jolly Farmer, his wounded knee had turned septic.

That night's match – which he won incidentally – was the last time Brother Reg was seen alive. The following morning he was found face down by the side of the road, having crawled his last. It was thought at first that Reg had been mugged or perhaps been the victim of a hit and run accident, but police forensics proved otherwise. They were able to match the wound to his head with a nearby bottle of Rasputin vodka which had been carelessly flung out of a car window.

Brother Reg's funeral was a celebration of his faith, his life and his darts. It was attended by exactly 180 monks, who later went on a pub crawl, which is almost certainly what he would have wanted.

RON AZY

Football

Few people in sport have dreamed bigger dreams than Ron Azy. Yet for a hundred years this football pioneer has been largely overlooked, even in the south-west, where he was born and raised. One has to wade through more than 800 pages of the *Devon Compendium* – that otherwise reliable source of sporting information on the clotted cream capital of England – before Ron Azy's name is mentioned in a solitary footnote. It could be said that he is one of sport's unsung heroes – but for the fact that there was a song about him:

> Ron Azy, sailed by
> Let fly, bull's eye!
> Waves high, stayed dry
> And still won the cup tie.

An apprentice stove-pipe welder in the Devon village of Meachem, Ron Azy was attracted to football from the moment he first saw an engraving of the sport in the *Bristol Evening Telegraph*. The year was 1890 and Ron would have been about fifteen at the time. In those days football did not penetrate into the furthest south-western corner of the country, petering out roughly near Yeovil. Rugby dominated the counties of Devon and Cornwall, but Ron Azy, his youthful enthusiasm kindled by the image of swanky, well-to-do men with bristly moustaches, determined to change things. So, he took a day off from welding stove pipes, caught the bus to Bristol and brought the first football back to Devon. Within a matter of weeks, Ron had set up the North Devon Works League. It was founded on very strict principles – the chief one being that clubs were tied to places of work, and teams had to comprise genuine employees. Stove-pipe welding was a thriving concern in Ron Azy's quiet little corner of north Devon and in no time at all – or three years to be precise – the Meachem Stove Pipe Welders had racked up three successive league titles. Their closest rivals, the Combe Martin Electroplating Institute and the East Creek Hospital Rontgen Ray Operatives, were some way distant.

However, Ron's success with Meachem did not last long. Advances in the world of plumbing, namely the introduction of capillary joints which meant that pipes could be fixed together without having to be welded, turned the stove-pipe world on its head. The other teams in the North Devon Works League watched with interest as Ron Azy's welders drifted away, one by one, to find other jobs. Then, sensationally, after a cup tie against the Ilfracombe Copper Bottomers, the father of Devon football was accused of contravening his own draconian rules. One of Azy's team was not a bona fide stove-pipe welder, it was alleged, and had been drafted into the team under false pretences. Ron refused to let the player submit to a welding test, at which point he and his team were summarily expelled from the North Devon Works League. Azy protested to the newly formed Devon FA, but his appeals fell on deaf ears – specifically, those of the hard of hearing Brigadier Sir 'God' Ken Smith, the tyrannical despot of Devon football.

Lesser men might have wilted under this onslaught, but Ron Azy was made of sterner stuff. He was determined he was going to play his beloved game and nothing would stand in his way. If he was no longer allowed to play football in Devon, then he would leave the county. On 12 April 1894, he welded his last stove pipe and resigned from his job. Using his savings he bought a job lot of timber, and together with some disaffected former work colleagues he began working day and night on the construction of an enormous wooden platform. When it reached the size of a football pitch, the wood was covered with a layer of turf and dragged into the sea off Bideford Bay. The following week, with the pitch anchored a few hundred yards from shore, and in front of 8,000 people crammed into the rickety wooden stand, the newly formed Azy United played their first match – a friendly against the North Devon champions, the Lynton Linoleum Cutters. Azy United won by three goals to nil.

Ron immediately applied to rejoin the North Devon Works League, but his entry form was rejected. Azy United were not, strictly speaking, a works outfit and as the floating football pitch was out at sea, and 'more than the distance a bottle of rum can be catapulted from the shore', it fell outside the territorial limits of Devon. Unabashed, Ron Azy set up a rival league. Teams could be constituted however they liked, he declared, and there would be no restrictions against turf-covered floating platforms, regardless of how far out to sea they were anchored.

Azy United won the inaugural North Devon Football League in 1896, although their triumph was not without controversy. Visiting teams invariably found the conditions on the floating pitch difficult, especially when there was an Atlantic swell. Many suspected that Ron Azy had put his stove-pipe welding past to nefarious use, pumping gas under the timbers to make the platform rock. Azy strenuously denied these charges, although a deputation from his bitter rivals, the Puttlehole Sub-Mariners, did claim to have noticed some unusually large and unexplained piping on the underside of the floating pitch during an exploratory dive.

By 1902 the island had been fitted out with seating or standing room for more than 20,000 spectators, together with what passed for decent living accommodation for a dozen men in Edwardian England. Ron Azy and his team bestrode not only the North Devon League, but the whole of football in Devon. His triumphs had been almost seamless, and scarcely a season went by without some cup or shield on display in the wobbly trophy cabinet. Pride of place went to the enormous Ogmandle Tophy, a silver cup that had been erroneously engraved and which was open to football teams from all over Devon. The only time his team had failed to win this magnificent prize had been in 1899, when the floating football pitch had broken its moorings in stormy weather and drifted down the coast into Cornish waters, where it had been impounded by the local authorities. Held under floating-island arrest for the whole season, Ron could only look on helplessly as the Ogmandle Tophy and the Lady Lindrum Memorial Shield fell to rival teams, and the name of the Ilfracombe Deep Sea Fishermen (Haddock) was engraved on the championship cup.

But the parochial nature of Devon football could not contain the restless genius that was Ron Azy for long. He'd watched from his soccer outpost as a fellow non-league club, Tottenham Hotspur, had won the FA Cup in 1901, and his team applied to join the competition in 1903. The Football Association turned Azy United down flat. Floating football clubs, they declared, were not welcome. A similar application, to join the second division in place of the struggling Port Vale, was also rejected. The Football League's letter of refusal, however, never reached the island.

On the afternoon of 4 October 1903, a surprised bunch of Barnstaple United players turned up in Bideford Bay and discovered that their opponents, Azy United, were not in their usual place – a catapulted bottle of rum beyond the low-tide mark. Ron Azy had slipped anchor and made off in the night with all hands and not so much as a word of farewell. It seems he'd attached makeshift sails to the terracing and, sensing favourable weather conditions, headed up through the channel, past Wales, Ireland, the west coast of Scotland and out into the Atlantic.

The floating stadium eventually landed in Stavanger, Norway, three days later. The main stand had suffered structural damage near the Hebrides while the club's inside-right had fallen overboard somewhere near the Orkneys. Ron applied for political asylum, which was granted, and the following year he asked if he could join the budding Norwegian football league. He might have succeeded, too, had it not been for a sole dissenting voice. It belonged to Lars Akselsen, whose own team, FK Akselsen, had fallen out with the Norwegian authorities and, for reasons too complicated to go into here, played on a wooden platform perilously suspended above Romsdal Fjord. So instead of competitive matches, Ron and his team – now augmented with a Norwegian inside-right – were forced to play a succession of exhibition games and challenges, which usually ended in their favour.

The team found Norway to their liking, and Ron married a local girl, Grete Skelbrod, a fish-gutter from Trondheim. Together they had a son, Ronald-Gunnar Azy, and that might have been the end of the story had it not been for the outbreak of war in 1914. Despite having lived abroad for more than a decade, Ron Azy felt the pull of his motherland in her time of crisis, and he told his team they should return to Britain. The floating football pitch could be put to good use in the service of king and country.

The team set sail for England in March 1915 to teary goodbyes in Stavanger harbour. That was the last time that Ron Azy, or his crew, or his infamous football pitch, was ever seen. The Atlantic seas were especially rough in the spring of 1915, and it was believed at the time that the stadium had sunk under a barrage of heavy waves. Thanks to the release of papers previously locked away under the Official Secrets Act, and having charted the wooden craft's position on a great big map, modern researchers have come to a different conclusion. They believe that Ron and his merry band were most likely caught in the middle of a ferocious sea battle between the German battleship, the *Graf Spee*, and the British warship, HMS *Devon*. Trapped between two heavily armed ships, each firing round and round of torpedoes and shells at each other, the flimsy wooden craft, with only a thin covering of turf to protect it, wouldn't have stood a chance. The Ron Azy Stadium, the former pride of Bideford Bay and Stavanger Harbour, would have sunk to the bottom of the sea. Or did it? Because for many years a

song persisted, hinting that Ron Azy might have escaped
after all and ended up on the other side of the world:

> Ron Azy, goodbye
> Shells fly, sailed by
> Shanghai, Brunei
> Ron Azy, didn't die.

DUNCAN MERRIVALE

Tennis

If you'd had the good fortune to watch a tennis match in Lancashire in the 1960s, it's more than likely your viewing pleasure would have been spoiled by the constant sound of trumpeting. It was a distinctive noise – not like the polished notes of a jazz band, or the call of elephants in the zoo. Instead, it was caused by the pollen-bothered nose of Duncan Merrivale, Britain's finest ever allergy-afflicted tennis player.

Born in 1953, great things were predicted for Duncan after he was kissed in the maternity ward of Blackpool General Hospital by Stanley Matthews, who was touring the town to show off his long awaited FA Cup winner's medal. Good luck would surely follow. Given a tennis racket for his sixth birthday, the young Duncan soon showed an aptitude for tennis and proved to be a master of the deceptive trick shot. He was able to impart so much spin with his warped wooden racket that most of his opponents were beaten before they'd even had their first swig of barley water.

In 1963, while the rest of the country was falling under the spell of Beatlemania, Blackpool went tennis mad.

Against all the odds, the ten-year-old Duncan Merrivale was crowned junior tennis champion of England. He won the title again in 1964, and in 1965 too – an unprecedented hat-trick. If his progress continued, experts reckoned, he would be a sure-fire bet to become the first British Wimbledon winner since Fred Perry in 1936. Sadly for Duncan Merrivale – and for fans of British tennis – it never came to be. There were those who speculated that it was being showered with flower petals that made it all go wrong for Duncan. Others contend that the barrage of pollen he endured had nothing to do with his allergies. Suffice to say that when he reached adolescence Duncan Merrivale's life – and the course of British tennis – changed forever.

It was during an inter-counties schools match in 1966 that tennis observers first gained an inkling – one might even say a sprinkling – of what the future held for Duncan. Playing against a boy he'd beaten the previous year with one hand tied behind his back (they employed an unusual handicapping system in the Lancashire schools' tennis league) Duncan had a sudden sneezing fit. As the spluttering worsened his eyes began to stream and, finding it impossible to continue, he retired from the game. When the same thing happened in the next tournament Duncan was referred to a specialist who declared that the boy had acute hay fever. He was given a course of medication, which appeared to alleviate the symptoms, and in his next game against J.G. Meadows, the junior champion of Buckinghamshire, Duncan showed all his old form and raced into a two-set lead. Then, unfortunately, the side effects of the medication took hold. He had failed to read the bottle's label properly. 'May cause drowsiness,' it said. 'Do not operate machinery or wield a tennis racket.' Sure enough, midway through the third set and a break to the good, Duncan went to his chair at the changeover and promptly fell asleep. No amount of cajoling from the umpire or being shaken by the net-cord judge had any effect, and Duncan Merrivale was defaulted.

Spurning the use of further medication, Duncan took the precaution of wearing a Second World War gas mask for his next outing, but the match referee refused to sanction its use and the Blackpool teenager had to leave it in his kit bag. Moments later he was sneezing his head off. Duncan's opponent, who was coincidentally the son of the match referee, won quite easily after that.

Despite a bad run of form – not to mention a badly running nose – Duncan Merrivale was entered for the junior championships at Wimbledon in 1969. Struggling in his opening game on Court Fourteen against the Brazilian number one, he was given a warning for producing a blue handkerchief. This contravened the club's policy of only permitting white kits – and hankies. Given some paper tissues Duncan continued to trumpet away in between points, until he was eventually disqualified for making noises that upset the Duchess of Kent – who was watching a match several hundred yards away on the Centre Court. There were tears in the boy's eyes as he left – a potent mixture of self pity and hay fever.

It was while he was on his way to the US junior championships later that summer that Duncan Merrivale finally found his salvation. Disembarking at New York he was handed a flyer which advertised the forthcoming American Allergy Affected Tennis Championships, to be held at Flushing Meadow. Duncan put his name down at once. It was to prove to be the finest gathering of nasally inconvenienced tennis players the game had ever seen. There was Lawrence 'Bless You' Bates, the 'Sneezer from Cincinnati'; Carlos 'Rhinitis' Rodriguez, the 'Mexican Trumpeter'; and Jean-Claude Michel, the self-styled 'High Pollen Count of Monte Cristo'. Towering above them all though was the figure of Sydney 'Snuffles' Johansson, the top-seeded American and rumoured to be the greatest player ever to have blown his nose during a tennis match. Duncan saw off his first opponent, Jack 'Drip Hooter' De Havilland, with very little effort. It made a big difference not having to worry about stopping for a sneeze every couple of minutes, and Duncan noted with pleasure that at no time did the umpire issue the dreaded command, 'Quiet please'. For the first time in what seemed like years he could enjoy his tennis.

After beating three more allergy-dogged players, including the redoubtable German, Albert 'Gesundheit' Schultz, Duncan Merrivale reached the final. Despite a display of gamesmanship from Johansson, who frequently waved his handkerchief just when Duncan was about to serve, the 'Blackpool Bugler' eventually prevailed in five loud sets.

Although he was fêted as the world's finest exponent of sneezing-interrupted tennis, Duncan Merrivale found there were few opportunities for an allergy-afflicted athlete in 1970s Britain. Instead, in 1976, he emigrated to the States and bought himself one of the new graphite tennis rackets with nylon strings. To his great surprise Duncan found his over-demanding nose stopped giving him problems. A thorough examination by an expensive American doctor revealed that Duncan had never suffered from hay fever at all, but instead had a highly rare and acute allergy to catgut.

It's always dangerous to speculate, but perhaps if artificial tennis strings had been around some ten years earlier Britain might have produced a champion who would have knocked Borg and McEnroe off their respective perches. We'll never know. The following year Duncan Merrivale retired from professional tennis and took up coaching. Today he works at a tennis centre in Detroit, teaching runny-nosed inner-city children how to play the game. The tissues he keeps in his kit bag are for his pupils' noses, not his own.

EDDIE BRIGGS

Football

By any sort of yardstick you might care to use, Eddie Briggs was not one of the great football managers. Even by the humble standards of Stockport County, the club where he was briefly in charge in 1924, he made few ripples on the pitch. But although he is long forgotten now as both a player and a coach, Eddie most certainly left his mark on the game. It's a legacy for which every member of the football community – whether a humble park player or an over-indulged millionaire – owes him a debt of gratitude, for it was Eddie Briggs who first coined the lion's share of the football clichés that are used today.

A tough-tackling half-back – first with Bury and then Stockport County – Eddie Briggs had an undistinguished playing career that garnered no medals. He joined Bury in 1912, just as they were relegated from the First Division, before being transferred to Stockport in the spring of 1914. When war broke out in the summer of that year, Eddie volunteered and joined his local regiment, the King's Own Stockport County Fusiliers. The Fusiliers were an unlucky bunch. They'd missed the infamous no-man's-land

Christmas Day match against the Germans, when they were caught in a surprise attack by the Kaiser's Own Borussia Dortmund Rifles. Badly injured by shrapnel in a war that hadn't been over by Christmas after all, Eddie Briggs was sent back to Stockport.

When the war finally did end he resumed his playing career, but the wounds to Eddie's leg gave him constant pain. The torment was alleviated by the radical new practice of massage, and Ted Green, Stockport's magic sponge man, pummelled Eddie's calf muscles prior to every game. On the one occasion he failed to do so, before a match against Lincoln City, the muscle went into spasm and, as no substitutes were allowed, Eddie Briggs had to limp through the match on the touchline. After the game he told a reporter from the *Stockport Herald* that he hadn't had 'the rub of Ted Green', which must have been misconstrued by the journalist for Eddie's words somehow emerged in the paper as 'the rub of the green'. From that moment, though, it became Stockport County's standard excuse whenever they lost a game, and by 1921 the phrase had passed into common football parlance.

Later that season, Eddie told the football writer from the *Stockport Messenger* that his muscles had fully recovered. To prove it he would be giving 110 per cent in his next match. This came as a big surprise to mathematicians as well as football fans, as prior to Eddie's comments no footballer had ever claimed that he would give more than 100 per cent effort.

In the summer of 1924, when Albert Williams stood down as manager, Eddie Briggs was given the job. It was something of a shock appointment – the *Stockport Telegraph* had been convinced it would be Bill Fairclough – but Eddie talked a good game and in his own words had got the job 'early doors'. What he meant was that he'd locked the doors to prevent Fairclough gaining access to the ground and then stood outside the chairman's office at half-seven in the morning. He told the waiting reporter from the *Stockport Argus* that as a manager he intended to take every game as it comes – that is, one game at a time – because there were no easy games in football. He also promised he'd make sure his team would 'set out their stall' – not a reference to formation or tactics, but the bring-and-buy raffle the players held outside the Golden Swan every Friday.

Unfortunately, Eddie's fine words buttered no parsnips and, far from his boys 'doing great', by mid-October Stockport County were rooted to the bottom of the Second Division. His forwards weren't scoring goals, and as Eddie Briggs told the *Stockport Times*: 'Goals win matches.' He chose a colourful way to show how easy it was to score goals – by taking a cow on to the Edgeley Park pitch and attempting to hit its backside with the nearest thing to hand, which happened to be the goalkeeper's banjo. Sadly for Eddie he missed the sizeable target from less than two yards. Humiliated in front of his own players, the writing was on the wall for Eddie Briggs. Specifically, that writing took the form of a note from the chairman, Sir Arthur Payne, which he'd pinned above Eddie's desk telling him that he'd better buck his ideas up or he'd be getting the sack.

In November Stockport had an important cup tie against lower league opposition, in the shape of Third Division Norwich City, a team renowned for their attacking flair and their bright yellow shirts. The match proved every bit the potential banana skin he'd told the *Stockport Chronicle* it would be. Although it was, as Eddie said, 'a game of two halves' (the previous season's experiment of dividing a match into three thirds having been abandoned), Stockport managed to lose both of them 1–0. When he was interviewed afterwards by the *Stockport Gazette* – as it happened during a localized outbreak of parakeet flu – Eddie Briggs told them he was 'as sick as a parrot'. But in truth, he was a good deal sicker than that. Eddie had caught rheumatic fever, and missed the next three games. By the time he returned, he'd lost the dressing room. Edgeley Park had been redeveloped during his absence and it took Eddie the best part of an hour to find it. When he did, he bumped into Sir Arthur Payne, who was busy pinning another notice to his office wall, informing Briggs he had one game left to save his career.

Stockport's next match was against the runaway league leaders Sheffield Wednesday, managed at that time by the wily Jimmy 'Ben' Nevis. Stockport could win, Eddie told the man from the *Stockport Bugle*, but they'd have 'a mountain to climb'. The match, just a week before Christmas, was played on a bitterly cold day, and Eddie Briggs – who hadn't really recovered from his illness – sat shivering in the draughty dug out, urging on his players. Against all the odds, Stockport County somehow prevailed. After the game, and clearly delighted with the result, he spoke to the press, mangling his grammar – a sure symptom of the after effects of rheumatic fever – as he did so. 'The boys done great,' he told the *Stockport Journal*. 'We was terrific.'

But Eddie Briggs himself was far from terrific. Sitting in the freezing cold had done him no good at all and by late evening he'd caught a very bad chill. He went home, but instead of going to bed, sat by an open window – perhaps the very window the form book had been thrown out of –

drinking tea laced with brandy. On the Sunday afternoon Eddie's condition worsened and – at the end of the day – he died.

ST JOHN FFOULKES-TTHOMPSON

Rugby League

St John ffoulkes-tthompson was one of British sport's most unlikely pioneers. Brought up in comfort in leafy Surrey, he came within a cigarette paper of becoming the first southerner to play rugby league for England.

Born in 1960, in Elstead, St John ffoulkes-tthompson came into the world with a silver spoon in his mouth. It wasn't that his parents were rich – his mother had gone into labour in the kitchen, her foot caught the cutlery drawer and the contents went everywhere. Contrary to his rather grand-sounding name, St John's family weren't posh at all. His parents were originally known as the Hasketts and had changed their name and called their son St John to give him a better chance of being accepted into a public school. As he was only a bank manager, Eton and the other top-notch schools were off limits to Mr ffoulkes-tthompson. But he and his wife persisted, and in the end they found a reasonably decent school, Fremling's, on the outskirts of Woking, that was sufficiently impressed by the family's hyphenated surname and St John's monocle, and let the boy in.

The school was not an especially academic one, and the

pupils spent most of the working day on the playing fields. Football was Fremling's sport of choice, and St John, being a rather well-built lad, found himself placed in goal. Though he was good at handling the ball, mobility was not St John's great strength – his great strength was his great strength – and he did not enjoy the game.

In 1973, St John's life took a dramatic turn when Mr ffoulkes-tthompson accepted a job in Yorkshire. A campaign to persuade the locals to deposit their money in the bank rather than stuff it under mattresses or wedge it behind the clock on the mantelpiece had reaped dividends. Mr ffoulkes-tthompson was sent north to oversee this grand new venture and took his family with him. St John was moved to a new school, Rumpney College, which was reputed to be the grandest of its kind in all of Yorkshire. Every morning its age old song, 'Eeh, by 'eck, up t'school', could be heard floating across the moors before the boys sat down to a fried breakfast. Teased at first by the other boys for being a soft southerner, St John disproved the first part of their taunts when he showed himself to be an expert at the Rumpney Ditch Game. This age-old and pointless school tradition involved the boys hurling themselves at one another and trying to push as many others as they could into the aforementioned ditch. St John's bulky stature – he was almost as wide as he was tall – combined with his natural strength meant he proved impossible to knock over. It was an impressive performance and gained him instant respect. The only bone of contention – whether or not St John was built like the proverbial brick outhouse – was set straight by Trubshaw from year nine. His discovery of a brick privy near Ilkley bus station with exactly the same dimensions as St John made the doubters eat their words.

Being ponderous, thickset and hard to knock over made St John a natural to play rugby league, and not long after his triumph in the Ditch Game he was elevated to the school team. He performed above expectations in his first game, against Mother Shipton's Academy, where he helped Rumpney College to an unexpected victory. Too slow to score tries himself, and too clumsy to kick, St John ploughed his way through the opposition players and made countless opportunities for his team-mates.

For the next few years St John ffoulkes-tthompson was a regular fixture in Rumpney's first team, which became one of the most respected rugby league schools in the north. He was even given the singular honour of being named the school captain when he reached the sixth form.

It might be supposed that such performances would have alerted the professional rugby league clubs to St John's talents, but this was not the case. They were certainly aware of him, but had their reservations. There had, of course, throughout the sport's history been many fine players of the game who didn't hail from the north of England – Australians, South Africans, New Zealanders and Fijians – but scarcely a single one born south of Coventry. Some years earlier Wakefield Trinity had had a player from Bristol – Jess Holscombe – but 'Big Southern Jessie', as the fans dubbed him, had found the pressures of the game too great, and quit. No one wanted a repeat of that unfortunate episode.

At the last minute though, just when it seemed as though he would have to take a proper job, St John ffoulkes-tthompson was offered a trial with struggling Featherstone Rovers. He did well, and in October 1979, just after turning nineteen, played his first game for the club. None of the crowd who saw his impressive performance in the 24–16 win over Hunslet had any idea that St John was a southerner. The club kept the information secret, and for the next few years St John knuckled down to his job and became a well-respected player.

In 1983, with the club already qualified for the Rugby League Challenge Cup Final, St John received a letter from the England selectors, inviting him to train with the squad. It was fantastic news – but on his way home that evening after a celebration drink at the working men's club – disaster struck. While negotiating his garden gate, St John was bitten on the leg by a whippet. At first he thought nothing of it – he had, of course, faced up to far more formidable opponents during his rugby league career – but when the wound failed to respond to conventional treatment, St John's friends began to worry. Emergency supplies of his favourite Eccles cakes and bread and dripping only seemed to worsen his condition.

At a loss as to what to do, St John was packed off to his parents, now returned to the family home in Surrey. No sooner was he there, scoffing cucumber sandwiches and smoked salmon, than he began to recover. Once back to full fitness he returned to Featherstone, planning to train for the Challenge Cup Final. It was not to be. The moment he arrived back in Yorkshire St John began to deteriorate again and he took the next train back to Surrey. When the pattern repeated itself, the unfortunate St John ffoulkes-tthompson was forced to sit out Featherstone Rovers' big day and watch their magnificent 14–12 triumph over Hull on his parents' television set in Elstead.

Since 1983, St John ffoulkes-tthompson has lived a life confined to the south of England. Every time he attempts to head north to Yorkshire he breaks out into a terrible rash, the true nature of which has baffled medical science. He did try to set up his own rugby league franchise in Surrey, but with insufficient local support it was doomed to failure. These days he's most likely to be seen behind the wheel or the counter of his burger van, touting his wares. The sign on the side, 'St John's Reet Good Grub', is unmistakable. He travels extensively across the south of the country, and does a roaring trade selling tripe and onion ciabattas and black pudding baguettes to Yorkshiremen exiled far from home. Not once has he ever ventured further north than Coventry.

TA'NEESHA FONTAYNE

Judo

Ta'Neesha Fontayne might have been lost to the world of competitive sport had it not been for a chance, and rather bruising, encounter. It was on an overcast and otherwise unremarkable September morning in 1987, when Ta'Neesha, a sales assistant at Dunmoore's Department Store, in Leicester, spotted a customer appearing to cut the security tag from a dressing gown. Suspecting that he was about to make off with it, Ta'Neesha gave chase, flipped him on his back and pinned him to the floor. Far from being angry at his treatment – he claimed he'd been innocently looking at the washing instructions – the victim was delighted. He introduced himself as Geoff Smeales, the head of the Leicestershire Judo Association, and once he'd struggled to his feet and the numbness in his shoulder had worn off, he invited Ta'Neesha to join his judo club. He slipped on the dressing gown and demonstrated a few holds in front of some appreciative customers.

Half an hour later, Ta'Neesha found herself out of work. While she'd been practising judo throws she'd

FORGOTTEN SPORTING HEROES No. 48

TA'NEESHA FONTAYNE

JUDO

left her till open, and someone had helped themselves to 300 quid. Not only that, but Smeales had walked out of the shop without paying for the dressing gown. Mr Dunmoore took a dim view of this and sacked Ta'Neesha on the spot.

Determined to bring Smeales to justice – and more to the point not having a job – Ta'Neesha joined the East Midlands Constabulary. She managed to combine her role as a WPC with her judo training to such a degree that she won a gold medal at the British Police Judo Championships in Carlisle. In between bouts she also helped the local force solve the Puzzling Problem of the Purloined Pearls, for which she received a commendation.

Ta'Neesha returned home in triumph, only to discover that in her excitement she'd forgotten to shut her front door properly before she left, and her house had been burgled. She asked her neighbour, Mr Collins, if he'd seen anything suspicious, but he said that he hadn't.

The following year in Swansea Ta'Neesha repeated her triumph. This time she'd made sure that her front door was well and truly secured and the windows bolted. She forgot to do the same to her locker, however, and when she came back to the changing room with her trophy and winner's medal she found that an opportunist thief had made off with credit cards and £27.66 from her handbag. Mr Collins, who'd been sitting in the audience, claimed not to have seen a thing. It wasn't all doom and gloom though – while in Swansea she'd helped the South Wales Police crack the Mysterious Mix-Up at Mapletoft Manor, for which she received a framed certificate and a kiss from the Chief Constable.

The police championships also doubled as trials for the

Great Britain judo team, and Ta'Neesha's performance won her a place in the squad for the 1991 European championships, in Poland. Out of pocket and close to uninsurable, and only too aware that every time she went off to compete she ended up being burgled, Ta'Neesha declined the invitation. It took some pleading from her boyfriend, PC Ashley Johnson, plus a nice box of chocolates, before she changed her mind. He promised he'd stand guard outside her front door while she was away so, with her mind at rest, Ta'Neesha headed off for Poland.

It was a very high standard of competition, and Ta'Neesha did remarkably well to come away with a bronze medal. Perhaps she would have performed even better had she not taken time out from her busy schedule to help the Warsaw Police crack the case of the Bamboozling Business of the Bakelite Buddha.

Ta'Neesha came home to discover her boyfriend had kept his promise, and the house was thoroughly secure. Too secure, in fact, as the smell that greeted her when she opened the front door indicated. In her hurry to compete, she'd forgotten to give Ashley a key, or to leave any food for Terrence, her pet hamster, and the unfortunate animal had died. She would have referred to it as the Regrettable Repose of the Recumbent Rodent, but she was far too upset.

Heartbroken, Ta'Neesha Fontayne announced her immediate retirement from judo. Reluctant to leave home, and refusing all offers of a replacement hamster, she instead threw herself into her police work. The Olympic Games, the World Championships and the Commonwealth Games all passed by without her. It was only late in 1994 that something happened that made Ta'Neesha change her mind. She was watching an episode of *Crimewatch* – required viewing for the Leicestershire Police Force – when she saw a photofit she recognized. The face of the man who Nick Ross said was responsible for a series of thefts at the Scottish Open Judo Championships was that of her old nemesis, Geoff Smeales. She grabbed her judo kit and an entry form and caught the first train to Stirling.

Despite having been in retirement for two years, Ta'Neesha had lost none of her old guile, and progressed serenely through the tournament. In between bouts she used her deductive brilliance to track Smeales to a small hotel near the centre of town. He tried his best to escape, but Detective Sergeant Fontayne caught him with a spectacular throw which sent him hurtling down the stairs – making it one of the few occasions when a suspect's injuries really have been sustained that way.

That, alas, was the only success of Ta'Neesha's trip to Scotland. She lost in the semi-finals, and failed to help Strathclyde Police make a breakthrough in the baffling Non-Alliterative Case of the Electrocuted Psycotherapist. What's more, when she got home she found she'd been burgled again. This time she'd forgotten to secure the back door properly.

That, however, was the last crime that Ta'Neesha suffered, as a few weeks later, the East Midlands Constabulary announced they'd got the man responsible. The affair known as the Recondite Riddle of the Repetitive Robberies had finally been solved. It turned out the culprit was Ta'Neesha's neighbour all along, Mr Collins. Thankfully she was able to recover most of her stolen goods apart from the £27.66, which he'd spent.

These days Detective Inspector Ta'Neesha Johnson is a

happily married mother of three. She and her family live in a pleasant house on the outskirts of Leicester with no pets, and very secure doors.

COLIN BLACKWALL

Ice Skating

Most visitors to Ballycastle in Northern Ireland head straight for the beautiful beach. If it's raining or a bit chilly, they might go to the world famous Museum of Washing. Were they to venture a little off the beaten track, though, and head past the arcades and the motorbike shop towards Eastley Street, they'd find the charred remains of a house: Number 114. This monument – or what's left of it – gives no indication that it was once home to the man regarded as the United Kingdom's all-time clumsiest ever sports star, Colin 'The Clunker' Blackwall.

A boy possessed of natural curiosity, Colin's inquisitiveness first got the better of him in 1975, when he was a little over four years old. He'd tiptoed into the school hall (when he should have been playing outside) so he could examine a spectacular display of children's handiwork. Approaching the stage he'd trodden on a loose sandal strap and blundered into one of the three trestle tables, bringing all of them down and ruining a whole term's work. On another occasion some careless footwork sent him tumbling through an open second-floor window. It was only his trouser waistband hooking on the catch that saved little Colin's life.

In 1976, the British government launched an initiative which it was hoped would pull Northern Ireland out of its increasing spiral of sectarian violence. What the province needed, ministers in London believed, were more whole-some activities to take their minds off the troubles – and what could be better than ice skating? So, the following year, in a bid to bridge the divide between Catholics and Protestants, dozens of ice rinks were constructed throughout Northern Ireland. In the end, as most communities could not agree, almost twice as many skating rinks were built as originally planned, with one for each faith in every town. Ballycastle, a forward thinking place, had only one – the Strandside Non-Sectarian Ice Skating Arena.

Under legislation, all children in the province were entitled to two ice-skating lessons a week – paid for out of the public purse. Regrettably Colin was forced to miss his first outing on the ice when he tripped over and grazed his knees on the way there. A week later, and with his legs festooned with sticking plasters, Colin Blackwall made it all the way to the rink. His teacher, Miss Phibbs, clearly expected nothing of the boy, but once on the ice Colin was a child transformed. While his classmates were blundering into each other, falling on their backsides or bawling their eyes out, Colin seemed to know exactly what to do. He glided gracefully around the rink without so much as a solitary stumble. He only came to grief when he stepped off the ice and lurched into Miss Phibbs, knocking off her spectacles and crunching them to pieces.

Colin won a book token at the end of the year for the

most improved pupil at the school. Aware of how uncoordinated he was, Mr Hunter the headmaster arranged to present Colin with his prize on the local rink. It was a thoughtful gesture, but Mr Hunter was a non skater, and had barely made it halfway across the ice before he fell, fracturing his arm in two places as he did so.

Within a year, Colin Blackwall was the Junior All-Antrim Ice Skating Champion, and by 1982 good enough to win the Northern Ireland title. At the age of eleven Colin had the world at his feet – provided his feet were sliding over the ice. The trophy, alas, never made it back to his house. Halfway down the corridor on the way to his dressing room he tripped over his feet, dropped the crystal vase on the stone floor and smashed it to bits.

At thirteen years, Colin Blackwall was too young to go to the Winter Olympics in 1984. So, like the rest of the country, he watched on television as Torvill and Dean skated their way to immortality. He was so thrilled with their triumph that he rushed into the hallway to tell his father, who was stripping paint off the banisters with a blow torch. Before he had time to open his mouth, however, Colin's foot connected with a canister of paraffin which went straight into the path of the blow torch. Half an hour later, 114 Eastley Street had burnt down. By the time Colin won his next trophy – the positively unbreakable Coleraine Cast Iron Skating Classic – the family were living in a caravan.

In late 1985 there was talk of a possible Winter Commonwealth Games, to be held in Canada. But when it was realized that none of the hot Commonwealth countries – in the Caribbean, Africa, Asia or Australasia – were interested, the idea was scrapped. Instead, Colin, now acknowledged as the UK's premier young skater, was invited to appear at the *Royal Variety Performance*. Dancing to a medley of hits by Kajagoogoo he wooed the crowd – which included the Queen and Queen Mother, who were both seen to clap appreciatively. Afterwards he was introduced to them, although the organizers made sure Colin stood on a specially constructed ice tray to reduce the risk of him stumbling into either of the royal guests.

Back home in Northern Ireland, though, the situation was deteriorating. Rival terrorist gangs now monopolized the supply of ice skates and refrigeration units. Parents became uneasy at the thought of their children going skating and, faced with dwindling numbers, many of the rinks were forced to close. A number of them reopened in other guises, Colin's own rink being re-developed as the Strandside Non-Sectarian Bingo Hall. Left with nowhere to skate, Colin Blackwall contemplated leaving the family caravan and moving to England, to train for the forthcoming Winter Olympic Games. He'd packed his skates and was just about to leave when a letter arrived informing him that the bingo hall was for sale. If he could raise the money, he could buy it and convert it back to its original use.

Colin was delighted. Friends suggested he might attempt a skating marathon along the frozen canals of Holland or even skate to the North Pole. The people in Northern Ireland, on both sides of the sectarian divide, were so proud of him he'd surely attract millions of pounds in sponsorship money. Colin told them he had a much better idea. Instead of skating, he would do a tightrope walk across the Grand Canyon wearing a clown costume.

It would perhaps be better, and kinder to his memory, to draw a discreet veil over what happened to Colin on that fateful day in 1987. Suffice to say that Colin 'The Clunker' Blackwall never returned home to collect that sponsorship money.

BRUNO WEBSTER AND
DR JONATHAN PARSLEY

Squash

In the late 1980s, when it was widely reported that Britain had more haunted squash courts than any other nation on earth, Dr Jonathan Parsley became quite a well-known media figure. He was the leading squash exorcist in all of England – if not the world – and had sent many a spirit packing.

In 1988, shortly after he'd famously rid the South Rochdale Badminton Club of its poltergeist, Dr Parsley paid a visit to a séance in Winchester. Tea cups rattled, a squash ball rolled ominously off a shelf and the words 'Bruno Webrest' were spelled out on the Ouija board. The name meant nothing to Dr Parsley, but it meant a great deal to his hostess that evening, Mrs Edwards. When her head stopped spinning she explained that Bruno Webster had been a noted Southampton squash player who'd won the Hampshire Open Championships eight times in the 1950s before he'd mysteriously disappeared.

That was more than enough to get Jonathan Parsley's ghost-hunting juices flowing, so he jumped into his

psychedelically painted van and headed down the M3 to Southampton. His first port of call was the LeisureWorld Squash Centre – a surprisingly dilapidated and empty establishment, bearing in mind that the sport was enjoying something of a boom in popularity. Keen to get to the bottom of this mystery, at first Dr Parsley came up against a brick wall – but that was only because he'd gone round to the back of the building where they didn't have a door. Once inside Jonathan Parsley questioned the only man there, an old caretaker, about Bruno Webster.

Back in the 1950s Webster, a painter and decorator by profession, had been the king of squash in the Southampton area. Eight times he'd won the local championship and in every single final he'd beaten the same man – Kenny Jarvis, an electrician. Nothing could match Webster's fitness or his dogged determination to retrieve every ball. Some said he used artificial stimulants or witchcraft (still controversial in 1950s Hampshire), while others claimed he played like a man possessed – possessed by a demon. When Dr Parsley wondered aloud why the LeisureWorld courts were all empty and if he could hire one for a game, the caretaker merely cackled and said that they were haunted by a vengeful spirit, adding that if he knew what was good for him he'd leave immediately and take up another sport like tennis.

Dr Parsley was not so easily deterred and returned to the squash courts later that night. His spirit busting instincts told him there was more to this mystery than met the eye – and besides, he just didn't trust the rather sinister caretaker. Opening the unlocked, but very creaky door, he inched his way along the darkened corridor, squash racket in hand. Just as Dr Parsley came to the first glass door, a terrifying wail tore through the leisure centre, while a ghostly apparition darted before his eyes and vanished through the wall. He mumbled a few of his favourite incantations but without any real belief because, despite all the evidence, Dr Jonathan Parsley was utterly convinced he had neither heard nor seen a genuine ghost.

The next morning he went to Southampton Central Library, dug out some old newspapers and began reading about the exploits of Bruno Webster. He and Kenny Jarvis had been friends and work colleagues, it seemed, a friendship that had been strained by Bruno's complete dominance on the squash court. Then after the Hampshire Open of 1959 there was no further mention of Bruno Webster. It seemed as though he had dropped off the face of the earth. Had a bitter Kenny Jarvis done away with his rival, bashing him on the head with a shovel and dumping his body in the Solent? The only clue was a photograph of the two athletes, one grinning and holding the trophy, the other crumpled in defeat. The closer the ghost hunter looked, the more familiar one of the faces became.

Dr Parsley headed back to the LeisureWorld Squash Centre and accused the caretaker of not only being the man behind the mysterious hauntings, but also of being Kenny Jarvis. The old man accepted the latter accusation, pointing to the name tag on his lapel that read 'Mr K. Jarvis', and confessed to being responsible for the ghostly goings-on.

As a young man in the late 1950s, Kenny Jarvis had felt his squash game was improving, and that it would only be a matter of time before he finally beat Bruno Webster. Unfortunately, two things then happened to deny him his chance. Firstly, squash went out of fashion and all the courts closed; secondly, Bruno Webster had decided to emigrate.

Now, in the late 1980s, squash was once again flavour of the month, and although he was too old to win the Hampshire Open himself, Kenny Jarvis had a couple of sons he was determined would become squash champions. So, to achieve his dream, he'd used all his old electrical skills to set up a succession of elaborate holograms and voice-activated traps to convince everybody the squash courts of Southampton were haunted by ghosts. With everyone frightened away, he could switch the machines off when his sons came to practise. It was a perfect plan but for one thing: Kenny Jarvis's sons couldn't give a monkey's about squash and both thought their dad was an obsessed old nutcase.

Dr Parsley considered informing the police about the caretaker's confession, but thought better of it. Aside from scaring a few gullible people, Kenny Jarvis hadn't really done anything so very wrong. In any case, the old caretaker promised to dismantle his ghostly machines, so the two men shook hands and that was that. The next morning Jonathan Parsley was gone – heading north to Kendal in Cumbria on the trail of a ghost who was haunting a swimming pool.

After he left England in early 1960, Bruno Webster settled in Australia. He worked on a variety of farms before buying his own in 1976. In all of Queensland no one else grows better pumpkins – or, as some people prefer to call them, squash.

INDEX